THE FINANCIAL SURVIVAL GUIDE FOR DENTISTS

Everything You Needed to Learn,
but Were **NEVER** Taught, in Dental School

Sam S. Shamardi, DMD

Contents

Part Two
Front-end and back-end essentials

Part Three
Owning your own Practice

Part Four
Facing your biggest fears...or a Pandemic

Appendix

Dedication

This book is dedicated to my mom for always encouraging me to follow through with whatever ideas and projects come to mind regardless of how ambitious they appear. While others would say no, you would always say, 'why not?' You pushed hard to make sure we took education seriously and sacrificed way too much of your time, happiness, and health for our benefit. You are an inspiration to me and my motivation for everything I do.

To my dad, for always reminding me that as difficult as school was, things would only get harder. You were right. Also, a special thanks for sitting me down at the start of my career to explain how to do my own bookkeeping and pushing me to pay more for my loans. Without your guidance, I would be at the mercy of the banks and loan carriers. You helped set a path of financial discipline that put me years ahead of where I otherwise would have been, and one I hope to share with others through this book.

To my sister, for always setting the example I ended up following. I basically did everything you did and liked whatever you liked since I was a kid, with the significant luxury of being able to watch from a distance and learn from your mistakes. It's hard to be on the front line, and you took many hits over time that I was able to avoid thanks to your warnings. Also, thanks for pushing me to specialize; I would not have survived a day as a general dentist and still can't stand the thought of making a temporary crown! I owe my career as a periodontist to you.

Lastly, to all my friends and mentors. Dental school and residency were the toughest years academically, but I never had more fun and met so many life-long friends. You each made the journey that much more memorable, and continue to fill a massive role in my life. I wouldn't trade these friendships for anything.

Preface

Monday, March 23, 2020 - Newton, MA

I should be at my Cambridge office today; gosh, my days there are always crazy with six to eight surgeries guaranteed, consults, post-ops…the works. Instead, I'm sitting here on my computer in my small home office, sporting the first beard I have ever allowed to grow (not a difficult task for me, but one I've never fancied having), and now in my second full week of self-imposed lockdown from this crazy coronavirus.

No, my offices aren't open nor am I treating patients outside of emergencies. But let's be real. How many dental emergencies are real emergencies? I spent my first week reading a great book and trying to generate new ideas to pass along to a partner company that is selling my first big entrepreneurial adventure; EarAid, the intelligent earplug.

Group chats and endless updates stream on my phone and the President has daily briefings with his corona task force. Having just returned from visiting my sister in Madrid just two weeks earlier where the virus was still in its infancy but Italy was on fire, I can already tell two things: one, we in the States have no idea what's coming and if we did, we would go on an all-out shutdown NOW; and two, given the first, I'm not going to be returning to work anytime soon.

I've always been comfortable living on my own and being independent, but this will take that to another level. Technically, I don't live on my own; my nearly 10-year old cocker spaniel, Luna, is always here acting like my shadow and keeping me company. They say dogs are like their owners, but watching her sleep most of the day and lick herself often I always wonder which specific qualities they are referring to.

If I follow her lead (with the sleeping only, of course), I will go mad, and I certainly can't watch endless TV for weeks. Time to go to work, lockdown style. For years I've probably been like most of you, complaining about not having enough time to do things, but now I have all the time in the world. I can't use that excuse anymore (damn!). But I know exactly what I want to do.

The weekend before this craziness started, I had some friends over for a BBQ. One is a practicing dentist of several years who started an office over a year ago, and the other is one of my perio residents where I teach part-time at Harvard. They are in two different stages in their careers, yet one topic they both agreed on and neither could understand was the lack of business education and preparedness for dental students. It's the one topic I've heard mentioned more than anything in my career, and the only one that never has an answer.

As a dental professional, some classic conversations never get old: stories of crazy patients, the drama between the office staff, insurance billing issues, things you expect in any people-based profession. But there is one conversation that always comes up that never makes sense at all: business management.

That's right, 4 years (or in my case 7 including residency), hundreds of thousands in tuition, endless exams, and hours in the lab. But what about business? Great, we graduate and are ready to practice the clinical side of dentistry, but we aren't ready to practice the business of dentistry. And as we soon find out (or will find out if you are still in school), the business side is what dictates our future.

How is that even possible? Surely, the practice management course we had in school is enough to prepare us for the real world, right? As you all know, that answer is a resounding NO, yet the responsibility is ours to bear. I don't care if you honored your boards, or were known to have the greatest MOD preps this side of the Mississippi because the reality is that until you begin to educate and prepare yourself for the business of dentistry, you will be swimming upstream for years to come.

Until now. Well, sort-of. It's March 23, and an outline I first created 6 years ago called "Dental Finance Outline" is open on my laptop. I take a peek and see it mentions some good things, but also needs a major facelift. But I've got plenty of time, and nowhere to go. There is a lot to add, and even more to look up, but the mission is clear: to hell with dental school not preparing us, and having to learn everything the hard way. Time to pay the system back.

No, this book won't teach you how to become a millionaire. It won't tell you what to say on your website, what to post on your Instagram, which stocks to invest in, or if you are better off being an associate or an owner.

What it will do however is give you the necessary tools to help you make those decisions for *yourself.* Without lectures, without an exam, and an extra year of your life. The material in this book will cover every topic critical to starting or restarting your career on the right foot. It's the answers to the exam we all spent hours trying to find instead of studying. It's what our practice management course was supposed to be.

The business of dentistry is no different than anything else in life; it's a game, and you want to have the knowledge to win. So, take control back, and get a head start. This is everything you need to know but were never taught in dental school.

PART ONE

Congratulations Doctor...Now let the games begin!

1

Ready or not... your first payment is here! (sort of...)

"Don't hate the player, hate the game."
~ Ice-T, Rapper/Actor (originally Chris Poole)

"Learn the rules, then break some."
~ Geoffrey Hunt, Ph.D., my childhood best friend

It's funny how fast things change; one second you are a student/resident, beholden to your faculty and institution, and then suddenly, with a piece of fancy paper, you are a Dr, ruler of your world.....and keeper of your debts.

I had barely finished unpacking the bags and boxes I had returned with after residency from Philadelphia to southern California when I already received my first two official letters in the mail. "Sam Shamardi, DMD" or "Dr. Sam Shamardi" both looked pretty cool, and I wasn't sure which one sounded better. I did know one thing though. What was inside those letters didn't feel quite as special.

One was from the alumni association asking for donations. Alumni association? I literally just got out! Now I'm an alumnus of two institutions, Tufts and UPENN, so I guess I'll be getting two of those. Giving back? I just paid 7 years of insanely high tuition, not including undergrad (thank you, UC public system), and they are already asking for donations? Interesting, but hey, I had a great experience so let's ride the wave and show them I'm grateful.

The second letter gave me pause: details for my first student loan repayment. Now, everyone's story is different; maybe you needed full loans, maybe your family kicked in enough to support your living expenses (thanks fam!) or maybe even more, but one thing is certain; the government and the private lenders don't care. You borrowed their money to pay that tuition, and now want their money back, and they want it now, sort of.

That's because they don't care when you pay them back. Either way, in the end, the House always wins. You see, there are deferments and grace periods, but make no mistake; whether you realize it or not, the clock is always ticking, and they are collecting. Like a cab waiting for you outside during a pitstop, your fare is going up whether you are riding or not.

Looks like I'm not going to rule my world after all! Or can I? Let's take control back from day one. To figure out how we need to first learn the rules so we can break them (figuratively, of course, sorry IRS).

Student Loans

The Essentials

To begin, you need to first understand How to read your statement. While you were in school and it came time to take out loans, more than likely, if you are like most dental students, you had no idea what any of the fancy terms or different types of loans meant to you. You may have gotten whatever you were "supposed" to get at the time. You didn't know better and just followed the script. I am not going to go too far into detail about the types of loans although I will discuss Federal versus Plus Loans since there is not much that you can do about that now. But I do want to discuss how to understand the repayment process now that you are finished with school.

Your statement should provide you with all of the information that you need to keep track of your account activity. The following sample identifies all of the important information including current balance, current amount due, and any amount that you previously paid and which is applied to this month's payment. This will be important as we discuss your repayment options.

Nelnet Statement Guide

https://www.nelnet.com/documents/marketing/pdf/Nelnet-Statement-Guide.pdf

Before we go any further, let's review some common terms that you should be familiar with to understand your statement and what it means to you.

Glossary of Terms[1]:

An academic year is one complete school year at the same school, or two complete, half years at different schools. For schools that have a year-round program of instruction, nine months is considered an academic year.

Credit - Credit refers to the amount of money you borrow and your ability to borrow to purchase goods and services. Credit is extended to you from a credit grantor with which you make an agreement to pay back the amount spent, plus applicable interest and fees, within an agreed-upon time.

Debt Consolidation - a method of debt refinancing that involves taking out one loan to pay off others.

Default - Default is the failure to repay a loan outlined in the agreed promissory note. Most federal student loan default occurs when a payment isn't made in more than 270 days. It can result in legal consequences and a loss of eligibility for additional federal student aid.

Deferment - a deferment is a temporary postponement of payment on a loan that is allowed under certain conditions and during which interest generally doesn't accrue on certain types of subsidized loans.

Direct Consolidation Loan - A Direct Consolidation Loan combines federal education loans into one loan for free via completion of the Federal Direct Consolidation Loan Application and Promissory Note. You will have a single monthly payment on the new Direct Consolidation Loan.

---

1 https://studentaid.gov/help-center/answers/topic/glossary/articles

Direct PLUS Loan - Direct PLUS Loans are federal loans that graduate or professional students and parents of dependent undergraduate students use to help pay for education expenses.

Direct Subsidized Loan - A Direct Subsidized Loan is a federal student loan for which a borrower isn't generally responsible for paying the interest while in an in-school, grace, or deferment period.

Forbearance - A period when your monthly loan payments are temporarily stopped or reduced. Interest will continue to be charged on your loans. Be aware that unpaid interest may be capitalized (added to your loan principal balance) at the end of your forbearance period.

Interest - Interest is a loan expense charged for the use of borrowed money. Interest is paid by a borrower to a lender. The expense is calculated as a percentage of the unpaid principal amount of the loan.

Lender - A lender is an organization that made the loan (borrower's school, bank, credit union, etc.).

Loan - A loan is money borrowed from the federal government or a private source like a bank or financial institution, and must be paid back with interest.

Principal - Principal refers to the sum of money lent, on which interest is paid.

Repayment - Paying back money you borrowed by making scheduled payments to a loan holder or servicer.

Unsubsidized Loan - An unsubsidized loan borrowed through the Direct Loan Program offers students a low, fixed interest rate and flexible repayment terms. It is not based on financial need. The borrower is responsible for paying all the accumulated interest until the loan balance is paid off.

Federal vs. Private

What's the difference? I do not want to assume that you understand what type of loan that you chose when you had to take out the loans so let's look at some of them to help you better understand what you have gotten yourself into.

Federal student loans are issued by the Federal Government and include options such as fixed interest rates and income-driven repayment plans. These options are not typically offered with private loans. The terms and conditions are non-negotiable but rather determined by law.

Private loans are made by private organizations such as banks, credit unions, and state-based or state-affiliated organizations. The terms and conditions are determined by the lender and therefore are typically more flexible yet can be more expensive than federal student loans.

Whether you choose federal student loans or private student loans, you have to pay back the money you borrow plus interest—whether you graduate or not.

There are three types of federal loans that are available to pay for college:

- Direct Subsidized Loans
- Direct Unsubsidized Loans
- Direct PLUS Loans of which there are two types: Grad PLUS Loans for graduate and professional students, as

well as loans that can be issued to a student's parents also known as Parent PLUS Loans.

In general, federal student loans provide additional flexibility in several areas than private student loans:

- Borrowers don't need a credit check to be considered (except for the Federal PLUS Loans for parents and graduate students).
- Some federal student loans offer income-driven repayment plans where the rate of repayment is based on the borrower's salary after college.
- Federal student loans allow the borrower to change their repayment plan even after they've taken out the loan.

It's important to consider federal student loans before you take out a private student loan because there are differences in interest rates, repayment options, and other features.

Private student loans can help you pay for college after you've explored scholarships, grants, and federal student loans.

- Private student loans usually offer the choice of a fixed or variable interest rate. Fixed rates stay the same, giving you predictable monthly payments. Variable rates may go up or down due to an increase or decrease to the loan's index.
- Private student loans offer different repayment plans—including options that allow you to make interest-only or fixed payments while you're in school. These in-school payments could lower your total student loan cost.

- Private student loans offer flexibility since they can be taken out by a student (often with a cosigner), parent, or creditworthy individual (e.g. guardian or another relative).

What are PLUS loans

Direct PLUS Loans (also known as grad PLUS Loan) are federal loans that are made to graduate or professional students. PLUS loans can help pay for education expenses not covered by other financial aid.

- The U.S. Department of Education is your lender.
- You must not have an adverse credit history. A credit check will be conducted. If you have an adverse credit history, you may still be able to receive a PLUS loan if you meet additional requirements.
- The maximum PLUS loan amount you can receive is the cost of attendance (determined by the school) minus any other financial aid received.

Repayment timeline

How long do you have to repay?

For federal loans: Once you graduate, your federal student loan goes into repayment immediately. In most cases, however, you have a six-month grace period before you are required to start making regular payments.

Note: When your loan enters repayment, your servicer will automatically place you on the Standard Repayment Plan and will provide a loan repayment schedule stating when your first payment is due and the amount. This information as well as the number and frequency of payments is available on your billing statement. You can request a different repayment plan at any time. If you signed up for electronic communication, pay attention to your email. Most loan servicers send an email when your billing statement is ready for you to access online.

For a PLUS loan: You don't have to start making payments until six months after you graduate. During any period when you're not required to make payments, interest will accrue on your loan. You may choose to pay the accrued interest or allow the interest to be capitalized (added to your loan principal balance) when you have to start making payments. Your loan servicer will notify you when your first payment is due.

General repayment schedules

Standard Repayment. Under this plan, you are required to pay a fixed monthly amount for a loan term of up to 10 years depending on the amount of the original loan amount. There is a $50 minimum monthly payment.

Extended Repayment. Similar to standard repayment in that it requires a fixed monthly payment, the difference with extended repayment is that it allows for a loan to be repaid over a longer period between 12 and 30 years depending on the amount originally borrowed. Stretching out the payments over a longer-term reduces the size of each payment, but increases the total amount repaid over the lifetime of the loan.

Graduated Repayment

Unlike the standard and extended repayment plans, this plan starts with lower payments which gradually increase every two years. The loan term extends between 12 to 30 years depending on the amount originally borrowed. The monthly payment can be no less than 50% and no more than 150% of the monthly payment under the standard repayment plan. The monthly payment must be at least the interest that accrues and no less than $25.

If you are interested in paying down your loan early or more aggressively, all Federal education loans allow prepayment without penalty. For loans that are not in default, any excess payment is applied first to interest and then to principal. However, if the additional payment is greater than one monthly installment, you must include a note with the payment telling the processor whether you want your prepayment to be treated as a reduction in the principal. This is the preferred option since it will reduce the amount of interest paid over the lifetime of the loan. Otherwise, the government will treat it as though you paid your next payment early and will delay your next payment due date as appropriate.

Whether you have a federal or a private student loan, an interest rate is the rate charged to borrow money. It's calculated as a percentage of your Current Principal and would have been established when you first took out the loan.

There are two primary types of interest rates: fixed and variable

A fixed interest rate is an interest rate that stays the same for the life of the loan. A variable interest rate is an interest rate that may go up or down due to an increase or decrease to the loan's index. Federal student loans only offer a fixed interest rate. Private student loans generally offer a choice of fixed or variable rates. Your student loan interest—both federal and private—may be tax-deductible. The type and rate of interest that applies to your loan is available on your billing statement and is an important factor in your repayment options.

Interest rate significance

The amount of interest paid over the life of repayment of the loan can and will increase as the term is extended. This amount could certainly be significant depending upon the agreed-upon interest rate. To avoid paying more in interest charges, it is important to pay more than the recommended or minimum payment to any lender. In other words, longer repayment periods and smaller principle payments mean paying more over time. Ideally, you should pay as much as you can upfront.

Time factor

How is time a factor in your repayment schedule?

The longer the repayment period, the more interest that you will pay to the lender. In other words, you pay significantly more! For example, if you took out a $400k loan, you could end up paying $625k in principal and interest by the time you have finished repaying the loan.

The government automatically puts federal student loans on a 10-year repayment timeline, unless you choose differently. If you can't make big extra payments, the fastest way to pay off federal loans is to stay on that standard repayment plan.

Federal loans offer income-driven repayment plans which can extend the payoff timeline to 20 or 25 years. You can also consolidate student loans which stretches repayment to a maximum of 30 years depending on your balance.

If you don't truly need these options and can afford to stick with the standard plan, it will mean a quicker road to being debt-free.

What if you aren't ready/financially capable yet (or ever)?

As a recent graduate, you are more than likely in the same position as millions of other recent graduates. You do not have a job yet in dentistry and therefore, have no means of repaying your student loans yet. There are several options.

Flashback fall 2010: Corona del Mar, CA

My graduation honeymoon was over; a few months off, a puppy in training, and remembering how fun it was living at home again. Time to go to work! The only problem was, it was hard to find a job! I thought it would be easy; surely people everywhere were looking for a periodontist. Months passed, some opportunities came, but not enough to keep me busy full-time, much less to begin paying thousands each month in loans.

Real-world panic started setting in. I did my first and only bout with shingles soon after. Next thing I knew, I was requesting my second deferment in a row, and a new reality crept in; the real world wasn't taking any prisoners. What if I kept having to defer? What if even once I found work I still wasn't earning enough to pay my bills *and* my loans? Was there anything else I could do? I never knew it at that time, but the answer is *yes.*

Deferment

If you're in a short-term financial bind, you may qualify for a deferment of your loan or a postponement of repayment. In most cases, interest will accrue during your period of deferment. This means your balance will increase and you'll pay more over the life of your loan. If you need to defer your loan, consider paying the interest that accrues during that period, so that you can avoid some of the consequences.

On the other hand, if you choose to request a student loan deferment, you won't have to make principal and interest payments during your deferment period. Your interest will continue to accrue (grow) while your loans are deferred, and at the end of the deferment, any unpaid interest will capitalize (be added to your loan's Current Principal). This can increase your total loan cost. If you can pay your accrued interest before it capitalizes, that can help keep your total loan cost down.

Maximum deferment time

The maximum deferment period is typically 3 years or 36 months. You can usually defer in 6-month increments and it doesn't have to be continuous. However, depending on what type of loan you are deferring, you may still accrue interest during the deferment period which is not good. If possible, try to consider the deferment of subsidized loans only (since the interest does not accrue). Worst case, if you cannot afford the repayment options at the moment, then go with the options below:

If you are claiming financial difficulty (on a 30yr loan), you have four income-driven repayment (IDR) options given you have a federal loan. These options do not apply to private loans.

Common characteristics of income-driven repayment options (federal loans only):

- A monthly payment determined by your income, family size and debt load
- Loan forgiveness after a certain repayment period (20 to 25 years)
- An annual review of your income, family size and debt load (meaning your monthly payment can change each year)

- Federal income tax may be owed on your forgiven balance at the end of the repayment term
- An often-higher total interest paid over the life of the loan

1. PAY AS YOU EARN (PAYE)

   If you're struggling with high student loan payments, switching to the PAYE plan could help make your monthly payments more affordable. PAYE is an income-driven repayment plan for federal student loans. For qualifying borrowers, the repayment plan limits payments to 10 percent of discretionary income.

   At the end of a 20-year repayment term, any outstanding loan balance is forgiven as long as no payments were missed during the term. PAYE differs from traditional Income-Based Repayment (IBR) because, depending upon the date your student loans were initiated, PAYE may cap loan payments at a smaller percent of income than IBR.

   This means monthly payments would be lower under PAYE. PAYE could also result in earlier loan forgiveness and better interest benefits for subsidized loans. If you qualify for PAYE, it is always superior to IBR. However, qualifying for PAYE is more challenging, and loan consolidation may be required before you apply.

2. REVISED PAY AS YOU EARN (REPAYE)

   The Revised Pay as You Earn Plan was introduced in December 2015 and is the newest option for income-driven repayment plans. Direct Loans, Stafford Loans, and Graduate PLUS Loans are eligible for REPAYE, as well as other non-parent federal student loans that are consolidated into Direct Loans.

Monthly payments are set at 10% of your discretionary income. (It is important to note that there's no upward limit on how much those payments might be.) Additionally, REPAYE offers student loan forgiveness after 20 years for loans originated for undergraduate studies and 25 years for loans taken out for graduate studies.

A REPAYE may be of interest to you if you are: single, have no graduate school debt, expect a higher future income, or don't qualify for the other options mentioned.

REPAYE also includes a student loan interest subsidy that can be a huge benefit for borrowers with monthly payments that don't cover interest charges. If they are on REPAYE, 100% of unpaid interest each month is paid for on subsidized loans; 50% of unpaid interest is subsidized for unsubsidized student loans for the first three years. After that, it covers 50% of the difference for both loan types.

Thus, say you qualified for $0 payments with this loan. Then each month for three years the government would pay half of your subsidized loan interest and all of your unsubsidized loan interest and would continue paying half of each beyond three years.

3. INCOME-BASED REPAYMENT (IBR)

Instead of payments being determined according to your student loan balance and interest rate, the amount due each month is directly connected to your income at the time. The plan takes into consideration income, family size, and location and determines payments as a percentage of your discretionary monthly income, typically 10% to 15%. This calculation depends on when your loans were disbursed.

You may be curious about this term "discretionary income" and in fact, may be wondering when you will have some. Your discretionary income is calculated as the difference between your adjusted gross income and 150 percent of the annual poverty line for a family of your size and in your state.

To qualify, your monthly student loan payments under the IBR plan can't equal or exceed what your payments would be under the 10-year Standard Repayment Plan.

Federal student loans eligible for IBR include:

- Direct Subsidized and Unsubsidized Loans
- Direct Graduate PLUS loans
- FFEL Consolidation Loans
- Direct Consolidation Loans

4. INCOME CONTINGENT REPAYMENT (ICR)

If you have applied for the other plans but were rejected, the Income-Contingent Repayment Plan may be your next best option for reducing your monthly student loan payment. It's the only IDR plan, for example, for which Parent PLUS Loans are eligible though you will have to consolidate these loans first.

Monthly payments are set as the lesser of either 20% of your discretionary income, or monthly payments when the loan is amortized over 12 years. ICR also offers student loan forgiveness after 25 years.

While there are some major benefits to enrolling in an income-driven repayment plan, there are some potential drawbacks as well that you need to keep in mind.

The repayment period for ICR is 25 years. After that, your remaining loan balance is forgiven (if there's anything left). However, note that any forgiven debt under ICR is considered to be taxable income. That means even if you do achieve loan forgiveness, you could be facing a steep tax bill in a quarter-century.

Your monthly payment amount under the ICR plan is calculated as the lesser of:

- 20% of discretionary income
- What the payment would be on a fixed, 12-year payment plan, adjusted according to income

Depending on your income, payments could end up higher than with the standard repayment plan.

The interest rate for the ICR plan is fixed for the life of your loan. If you first consolidate your loans, your interest rate through ICR is the weighted average of the interest rates on the loans included, rounded up to the nearest one-eighth of 1%.

Pros of Income-Driven Repayment plans

- Lower monthly payments. If you have low income compared to the amount that you owe in student loans, an IDR can help to make monthly payments more manageable until you can increase your income.

- Adjustable payments depending on the overall situation. Since the monthly payment due is calculated based on income, family size, and location, this amount may change depending upon your current situation. You can ask the lender to recertify your plan when appropriate. If warranted based on circumstances, the amount due may be $0.

- Student loan forgiveness. Based on the type of income-driven repayment plan you qualify for, you may be eligible for student loan forgiveness after 20 to 25 years of **on-time** payments. Remember that the forgiven balance will be considered taxable income when forgiven.

- Public Service Loan Forgiveness (PSLF). PSLF allows for student loan forgiveness after 10 years of on-time payments. Also, loans forgiven through the PSLF are not considered taxable income and therefore are not taxed. Dentists, dental assistants, and hygienists who work for a nonprofit or public service agency are eligible for this plan.

Cons of Income-Driven Repayment plans

- Longer repayment period. A Standard Repayment Plan takes typically ten years to repay the loan. An IDR plan stretches the payment to 20 or 25 years.

- Taxable income. Any student loan balance that is forgiven is considered taxable income and will come with a very sizable tax bill.

- Higher interest. While lower payments are great for your pocket now, you will be accruing interest over a longer period, increasing the overall amount paid.

- Increased loan balance. In most cases, a reduced monthly payment means that interest is not paid monthly but rather is tacked onto the end of the loan increasing your overall loan balance.
- Documentation. Lenders and financial institutions will automatically send you a Standard Repayment Plan. If you are looking to reduce your payments due to financial difficulty, you will have to apply for IDR plans and recertify your income every year.
- Eligibility. Federal student loan borrowers must qualify for an IDR plan. In some cases, federal student loans must be consolidated for borrowers to qualify for an IDR.
- Income. An IBR plan is determined by a percentage of your income. If 10 percent of your income is higher than your monthly payment on a Standard Repayment Plan, then you may not qualify for an IBR. Loan repayment and IBR eligibility may be determined by your combined household income if you are married.

To qualify for any of the Income-Based Repayment plans, you must demonstrate financial hardship, and once eligible, the rates are recalculated every year by the plan servicer.

Practical situation

When considering buying a business or building a practice from scratch, consider applying for an income-based repayment plan as you will already be financially stretched. You can defer monthly payment to keep your overhead to a minimum as you start the practice.

How you can lose the battle, but win the war: Tactics to repay loans faster

"The best defense is a good offense"
~ Dan Gable, Olympic gold medalist in wrestling and the most successful coach in history; personal record: 299–6–3, with 182 pins

Flashback fall 2012: Boston, MA

Life was much better now. I was working full-time and was back in Boston again where I always really wanted to be. (And yes, I'm fully aware that for most people the order should be in reverse geographically.) I was *finally* earning decent money and felt like I could actually start seeing some numbers slowly grow in my bank account. Time to buy a new car or a fancy watch, right? Not quite, and fortunately, my dad made sure of it.

Little did I realize, but all those "suggested" payments I was sending each month for my loans were barely making a dent on my balance. I was paying thousands; the balances had barely even changed by hundreds. Why? Because most of what I was paying was only going toward the interest, not the principal. To truly make a dent in my balance, I had to pay more than the "minimum amount due" written at the bottom of each payment bill. *A lot more.*

My dad explained that thanks to the insanely high interest rates many of my loans carried (6 – 10%), I could make those minimum payments for the rest of my career and *still* owe hundreds of thousands. Why pay more of your hard-earned money to the government in the long run, when you could pay more in the short run and pay everything off in half the time?

A few phone calls and some calculations later and I was feeling poor all over again, but this time, I was taking control back.

I may have been losing the battle on the front end, but I was winning the war.

Doubling down

If you are interested in doubling down, getting out from under the weight of your student loan debt, let's look at several ways to go about doing this.

Make extra payments the right way.

There's never any penalty for prepaying student loans or paying more than the minimum. You can make an additional payment at any point in the month, or you can make one larger payment on the due date. Either way can save you a lot of money.

But there's one big caveat. Student loan servicers, which collect your bill, may apply the extra amount to next month's payment. That advances your due date, but it won't help you pay off student loans faster. Instead, instruct your servicer — either online, by phone, or by mail — to apply overpayments to your current balance, and to keep next month's due date as planned.

Personal experience

Call your loan companies. Ask them what you would have to pay per month to cut the repayment time in half for each loan. See if you can afford it and if so, start doing that! Yes, the monthly amount will be much higher and feel like a gut punch, but what you are saving in interest and the long run is *substantial* and you can finish repayment considerably faster.

Refinancing/consolidation factors and limitations

Refinancing or loan consolidation is another way to reduce student loan payments and possibly save some money in the long run. By consolidating your existing loans into one single loan, with the expectation that it is at a lower interest rate, you can make one easy payment per month and hopefully reduce the overall interest paid over the term of your repayment plan. If your main concern is to reduce your monthly payment now, you can also consolidate your loans into a longer-term loan but this may increase the amount of interest that you ultimately pay.

Note: Only loans from private lenders can be refinanced. Federal student loan refinancing makes a borrower ineligible for IDR plans, deferment, and forbearance. Also, it's important to note that refinancing is performed by private lenders only.

Consolidating Loans

If you have several federal student loans, it is possible to consolidate them into one federal loan through the Department of Education. Although consolidation may be necessary to apply for an IDR, federal consolidation in itself will not reduce your interest rate. Instead, when consolidating loans, the new fixed interest rate is based on the weighted average of all loans being consolidated.

Depending on your case and how much you owe on each loan, it may extend the term of your loan to give you that much-needed monthly debt relief. But keep in mind, this can also work against you if you have more debt in lower interest loans. The interest rate of those loans will increase with the new fixed-rate via the consolidation. Thus, realize that consolidation of your federal loans may increase the amount of interest that you pay over the life of the loan.

Refinancing versus Consolidating Loans Which one to choose?

The answer to this question will depend on your personal situation and goals.

If you have the credit and income requirements to qualify for a lower rate, refinancing can save you money and help you become debt-free faster.

If you consolidate your federal loans through the government, you won't receive a lower interest rate, but you may qualify for loan forgiveness programs or income-driven repayment plans. Federal student loan consolidation won't save you money. In fact, it may extend your loan repayment schedule, increasing the amount of interest you pay long term.

For those who have specialized in the dental industry, your debt to income ratio is going to be really out of whack! Having more and larger loan amounts, you need to evaluate how you can best handle the monthly payments when just starting in your field. Consider consolidation and income-driven repayment programs, knowing that based on your specialty, your revenue and income will increase.

No matter the amount that you owe or your current situation, you should still pay additional toward the principal every month to pay down the debt faster and reduce the overall interest paid if possible.

Dental Loan Organizer and Calculator - DLOC

For currently enrolled dental students, graduates, and residents, I suggest taking a look at the website below and taking advantage of their loan organizer and calculator. Known as "DLOC" for short, this site will allow you to input all of your loan information, and after creating an account and answering a few brief questions, it will help you breakdown ALL of your loan information, including different payment scenarios and options based on potential income and timeframes.

This is a great tool for everyone in school and planning ahead and those who are just finishing and want to start organizing to get ahead. Chances are if you are reading this book, this will appeal to you directly, and I would highly recommend taking a look... you have nothing to lose and a lot of free information to gain!

https://www.aamc.org/services/fao-first/godental/

Personal Note:

As of now, March 2020, I still owe payments on my loans. Scary considering it's been a decade as of June since I graduated and a solid 9 years after beginning my first repayments. But a closer look tells a happier story; all of my high-interest loans have been completely paid off, and of what remained, I was able to get them refinanced with First Republic Bank for an insanely low interest rate of 1.95%. This means I can rest easy and glide my way to the home base. And I'm ***finally*** below 6 figures!

It's been a long journey for sure, and I still have a little more to go. But at the "recommended" pace I was following back then I still would easily owe $300k+ more at this point. A little extra money upfront each month makes a ***major*** difference.

During these years, I have been able to travel consistently for holidays and breaks, buy my first house, drive a good car, eat and drink well, and still put some money away in savings. My point is, despite the initial hardship of extra loan payments, it doesn't mean you still can't survive and live a good life.

NOTE - If you happen to purchase your own office, and maybe even a house, soon after graduation, it's likely you won't have the extra funds to pay your loans off at a higher payment, much less at the minimum. That's where the income-based options will come into play and give you breathing room and flexibility.

2

Essentials to know ***before*** *you sign on the dotted line*

"It's not personal Sonny; it's strictly business."
~ Al Pacino, The Godfather

"Always read the fine print"
~ anonymous

You are a signature away from joining an office. Congrats! You may have been looking for this opportunity for months or had a great connection through mutual friends; either way, the contract is the final thing holding you back from starting to live out your dreams and get your first paychecks.

Of course, you went to dental school, not law school, so all these pages filled with fancy terms you never heard of don't make much sense, but who cares because it means you have a job!

Besides, everyone seems friendly and honest so you are certain this is a good fit.

Perhaps you are right, perhaps not. Are you willing to bet your future on it? The test drive might be great, but now you need to talk numbers. Before you take the plunge, understand what all the language means and what pitfalls to avoid *before* you sign on the dotted line.

So, first of all, it's important to know what kind of an associate you will be. Will you be an employee or an independent contractor (IC)? In other words, will you be a W-2 employee or filing as a 1099 independent contractor? Each associate type comes with its advantages and disadvantages and we will touch on these as well as the things to watch out for relative to both. We will discuss what being an independent contractor means and how to establish yourself in detail in Chapter 3.

The following terms and definitions that will be discussed within this chapter will apply whether you are new to the dental field looking for a job or if you are a practice owner, considering hiring your first associate. We will discuss the latter in more detail in Chapter 6.

As an employee or what is commonly referred to as an associate in the dental profession

- You would have a fixed schedule that usually the employer controls. You would have all of the benefits that you should receive as an employee such as unemployment compensation, paid vacations, and health insurance.
- You would not be responsible for withholding or paying your payroll taxes; that would be your employer's responsibility. You would only be responsible for filing

your tax returns annually after receiving a W-2 form from the employer.

- You would be protected under federal laws such as minimum wage, anti-discrimination, overtime, etc.

From a prospective employer's perspective

- Being hired as an employee gives the employer "more control" over the schedules, more supervision, more general control of how or when the work is performed.
- As an employee, the employer owns the patient records.
- If they hire you as an independent contractor, it would be like hiring an expert or a specialist in an area that their practice lacks to enhance the services that their practice provides. For example, an orthodontist, an endodontist, or a periodontist.
- As an independent contractor, the employer would be saving a lot on labor costs because they wouldn't be responsible for any of those benefits that you would have as an employee. Keep in mind that oftentimes dentists are mischaracterized as independent contractors, when they're performing as employees, technically speaking.
- An independent contractor has the right to patient records or the right to copy them in case of litigation, malpractice, peer review, etc.

Independent contractor benefits

- As an independent contractor, you have autonomy over decisions such as managing your schedule and time.

- Managing your own finances and tax liabilities.
- It also allows you the freedom to build your practice on the side if you need to and build your own patient list.

Employee benefits

- Stable income stream in the form of a salary or hourly rate. It is common in the dental industry for employee compensation to be based on a percentage of production or collections.
- Benefits as mentioned earlier such as health insurance, worker's compensation, and the fact that you would be making contributions towards your future social security.
- Less responsibility

When trying to decide whether to work as an independent contractor or associate, carefully consider the following:

- Do you prefer a steady income or are you more aggressive, entrepreneurial, and want to have the ability to get your own patients and build up a little bit more aggressively?
- Do you prefer the safer approach of getting a steady paycheck every week/month?
- Do you want to market to other practices as well?
- Are the benefits that are being offered as an employee important or necessary to you and your lifestyle such as health insurance, etc.?
- Do you prefer to work in a more controlled environment with clear expectations and direction?

- Are you capable or able to go out and find patients or get referrals for the practice?
- Do you want to be responsible for your withholding?
- It is important to note that the choice of whether to become an independent contractor or employee is not always yours. In many cases, it is determined by the specialty that you are in as well as the type of office environment.

General Contract Basics

Note: This book should by no means be considered legal advice of any kind. It is intended as a guide for your personal use only. Be sure to consult an attorney that specializes in contract law to carefully review any contract before you sign it.

The following however is a list of things that you should look for when presented with a contract for employment or as an independent contractor.

Terms of agreement

Most contracts are on average 1-year contracts (but you need to know that if your contract terminates automatically, it may affect or negate certain rights or responsibilities even if your contract continues i.e. restrictive covenants which will be discussed a bit later). If you are an independent contractor, the contract (if you even get one) should clearly define the commencement and termination dates.

Compensation schemes as an employee or associate

- Salary: either weekly or better said probably bi-weekly, monthly, or per diem. That's the simplest way to be compensated when you are directly out of school.
- You would want to know if your salary includes any bonuses for exceeding production goals that they've given you.
- Commission basis which is how many dentists are paid.
- It could be based either on gross production or based on the net collection.

You could have a straight commission which would be a percentage paid across the board of either production or collection; or you could have a salary plus commission, in which case you would receive a base salary and a percentage of a commission base or goal. When first starting, many dentists are very comfortable with having this kind of guaranteed base salary so that they can have a few months to build rapport, get to know their practice, etc. but this depends upon your particular situation.

Compensation valuation

Most dental associates are paid on a percentage of production or collection.

Collection is based on many different factors including discounts, insurances, and the collection percentage itself which could depend on practice location and type. Ideally, you want a collection ratio of **95 percent or higher**. Offices that have collection rates BELOW 80% should be seen as a red flag. If they can't collect the money, and you are paid off collections, then, of course, you will not be paid the full amount for what you worked.

Production is based on what you've produced minus discounts, lab fees, insurance write-offs, lab remake fees, or any non-collected accounts. Lab fees are typically calculated as a portion of the lab bill equal to what you receive as compensation. In other words, let's say you make 35 percent of collections, then, you would pay 35 percent of the lab cost as well.

Average Percentage Pay for GP vs. Specialist

On average, a general dentist is paid 32 to 35% of collections or 30 or 32% of production.

For specialists, the average is usually between 45 and 50% of collections or 40% of production.

These rates vary depending on location, the type of procedures that are being done, and the method of payment that the patients choose.

Getting a percentage of production offers better clarity because it's easier to track every month and you don't get penalized if the front office doesn't do their job properly. However, most owners prefer to pay based on collections because it's better for their business. Also, it encourages associates to get clear consent when presenting treatment plans to patients.

This makes it tougher on the employee or IC to keep track of payments and income as insurance payments can lag for months. Therefore, you must be very careful and do your due diligence in accounting to keep track and make sure you are not being taken advantage of!

Ask for daily, weekly, and monthly reports; do some basic math of what you expect payment to be based on the numbers and see if it makes sense! Ultimately, it's YOUR money, thus YOU have to be responsible. If an office purposely or accidentally misses any payment, it won't affect them but WILL affect you....thus, you must stay on top of things!

The Deal Breakers

Restrictive Covenant

One of, if not THE most important part of a contract, the restrictive covenant is the area/distance which you will be prevented from practicing in after your employment is terminated. In other words, it is a covenant not to compete with your former employer when you leave.

It is important to understand the terms as defined by the contract where you can and cannot practice and the terms may vary depending on whether you are an independent contractor or employee. Some things to look out for include:

Distance: The distance in which you cannot practice will vary depending upon whether you are in an urban or rural area. Within a city, the distance will be very small compared to a rural area. If you are in a city center, the distance of your restrictive covenant could be very impactful on your decision to open a practice of your own so be sure that you pay attention to this number; make sure you don't handcuff yourself! For example, if you practice in a downtown area of a small city, do not sign a contract that limits the distance to be further than 2 miles if possible. In Boston, that would already nearly eliminate all city options!

Timeframe: While the timeframe will vary, typically the timeframe in which you cannot practice under this restrictive covenant is typically 1 to 2 years. If the employer is requesting to go beyond that, they should have very strong justification!

Note: It's generally much more difficult to enforce a restrictive covenant on an independent contractor rather than on an employee.

Non-solicit clause

A non-solicit clause is a typical part of an employment contract that prohibits you from contacting patients or customers or the staff after the end of your employment agreement. It is meant to help prevent stealing the practice's former patients or their employees.

Friends and family: Any patients that you have directly referred to the practice, including friends and family, should be excluded from the restrictive covenant and non-solicit clause, allowing you to take those patients with you to your own practice.

Red flags in Dental Contracts

- Transparency. A dental practice owner should be willing to share what former associates earned when performing the same type of procedures that you will be performing as an associate. If a practice owner doesn't want to share that with you, that should be a very big red flag that they have something to hide.
- Signing bonus. While some offices choose to offer a signing bonus, be careful if you've been offered an extraordinarily high signing bonus. This may be a sign of very high turnover and that it is not a stable practice.
- Excessively long notice period. While an average notice to terminate is typically 30 to 60 days, a notice period that is longer than 90 days should be a red flag and the owner must demonstrate a good reason for it. Also, the term for

both employer and employee should be equal, allowing either the ability to leave a bad situation if one exists.

- Geographic restrictions. If you are a specialist working in multiple locations, avoid any language in the contract that may restrict the location in which you can practice. This may be considered a shady business practice by an associate. Instead, it is preferable to have a 6-month exclusion clause before the restrictive covenant begins rather than a geographic restriction.

Dental associate agreements can be difficult to navigate and understand if you are not completely familiar with the language and terms. It is recommended that you work with an attorney to help you review the document before signing on the dotted line to avoid restricting your future opportunities, benefits, and salary potential. If you are already a dental practice owner, you must understand the ramifications of hiring your dental associates to protect yourself and your practice. If you are unsure as to how to find an attorney to assist you with legal issues relative to the dental industry, the ADA has published "A Dentist's Guide to Selecting a Lawyer".

Although I have touched on a few pitfalls in contract negotiation and discussed the difference in compensation for employees and contractors, there is quite a bit more information that you may need for your specific situation or practice. The American Dental Association has published a very well-written document that can assist you with many of your questions in this area. "Dentist Employment Agreements: A Guide to Key Legal Provisions"

Personal Note:

For reference, my personal experience with contracts has been varied due to my status as an independent contractor, and also because of having worked for different types of dental practices in different states.

First, when I started my career in California, I worked for a mix of both private multi-specialty offices and corporate. In the corporate office, I did have a contract and was paid via production. It made the math very simple: I went to work, at the end of the day I received a printed report of my daily production, and so doing simple math, I already knew exactly what my check would be. The hassles of insurances and collection were left to the company itself to manage, which was fine by me. The flip side was that the percentage was slightly lower, approximately 40%. Considering this was a high-volume style practice, the smaller percentage for production was a good trade-off in my opinion. My other private offices paid via collection, which was at 50%. My pay was determined by how good the front desk was at collecting and how well organized they were with insurance claims, etc. Unfortunately, insurance usually takes weeks to reimburse (for a good insurance company) so trying to manage my accounting was trickier though not too bad given I only had a few offices.

I didn't pay as much attention at that time to any restrictive covenant that may have been in place; all my offices were located far away from home, so even a massive zone of 10 to 20 miles would have made minimal difference to me so in that sense I wasn't worried.

When I returned to Boston where I am currently an independent contractor, I have no contract that I need to sign with any of my existing private offices, nor at this point in my career would I ever consider signing one (that would be a red flag). However, I did have some interesting scenarios.

First, I noticed at one practice that my overall paycheck was lower than what I expected. This was hard to notice at first since it was part of a larger group of corporate offices. However, after some digging around, I realized that the office's rate of collection was only hovering around 50%! That meant that regardless of how hard I was working, half of my efforts were a total waste of time! This is a prime example of where collection versus production comes into play; collection only works well when the office is actually collecting! My remaining practices were collecting between 87 and 98% as you would expect.

On a production basis, I would have been making more despite the lower percentage; collection at a higher percentage only really works for you if collection is above 90%. Needless to say, I quit that particular office soon after.

I have seen contracts with a very restrictive covenant of 2 to 3 miles. Now, if you work downtown, that is bad news as that pushes you out of the city for the duration of the covenant. So again, pay close attention to the number, where you live, and where you work. See if the numbers make sense or work against you and plan/negotiate accordingly.

Lastly, whatever you do plan everything based on the long-term. You never know what events may come up and if or when you may change your mind on your living and practice location. Don't ever have the "well, let's just start and see what happens" attitude as this may come back to bite you later. Plan ahead as best as you possibly can, putting yourself in the least amount of pressure positions in the future.

3

Employee versus Independent Contractor

"Control your own destiny or someone else will."
~ Jack Welsh - CEO of General Electric 1981-2001.
Named Manager of the Century by Forbes Magazine 1999

Unless you are already a practice owner or partner at this point (to be discussed in chapter 6), you will either be considered an employee or an independent contractor as mentioned previously. Each has very different implications, both for your taxes and for your ability to control the business side of your career.

That's not to suggest that one is better than the other, but rather to say they are as different as winter is between LA and Boston. What they have in common is they will dictate your financial present and future, and many other things in between.

While we looked at some of the differences between the two in the previous chapter, we will focus primarily on working in the dental profession as an independent contractor in this one. If you are planning to become an independent contractor, you have some serious homework to do.

As an employee of a dental practice, you receive a W-2 tax form, are paid regularly, and withholding taxes are paid on your behalf. Health insurance is typically covered by the practice owner but is something that should be discussed during the employment agreement process. Some practice owners may offer to cover other expenses like continuing education costs to employees including conferences, webinars, study clubs, etc. since these are all necessary for license renewal.

In some ways, being an employee of a dental practice may be simpler and provide more protection. For example, if a practice is sued, there is an extra layer of "protection" for you as an employee since the practice is required to have malpractice insurance (to be discussed in Chapter 4).

As an employee, you do not have to be concerned with tax deductions, insurance payments, or working at multiple locations. The benefit package may even include 401K retirement planning and/or a pension plan.

Conversely, as an Independent Contractor, the advantages of being an employee are some of the very things that you need to consider.

Definition: An independent contractor (IC) is simply someone who works for someone else, but not as an employee. For income tax purposes, you are considered a sole proprietor. The designation of "sole proprietor" is the default form of small business.

While you still get paid for your services as an IC, your payments are not a salary or wages but rather are considered business income which is deposited into a business checking account (yes, you should have a separate business bank account). You can take money out of the business as a "draw", but it is not considered a salary because you are an owner—not an employee. The amount you take out as an owner doesn't affect your taxes since you must pay tax on ALL the income of your business, whether you take it out or not.

Because you aren't an employee, the payments you receive from your business don't have any federal income tax withholding taken from them, and there are no deductions for social security or Medicare.

Of course, you can't get out of paying taxes, and you must still pay federal and state income tax on your income from your work as an independent contractor, through the business tax return. You will receive a 1099 form to be filed with your tax return as proof of taxable business income received. Taxes for social security and Medicare also must be paid; this combined tax is called self-employment tax for independent contractors.

Since you will not be making payments on your taxes payable through weekly or bi-weekly payroll deductions, you are required to make estimated tax payments to both the federal and state government in the form of quarterly payments.

When you are considering working as an independent contractor, you must also decide what type of corporation you will create. The goal is to create an entity that shields you personally along with your assets from legal issues (limited liability). You are in essence separating "yourself" from your business. This protection is vital as an IC. For dental employment contracts, be sure to use the name of your business (Doing Business As name) rather than your own name to guarantee this protection.

Step by step process to creating a business:

1. Choose an available business name that complies with the Secretary of State's corporation rules. Go to the Secretary of State website in your state to confirm available business names.

2. Appoint the initial directors of your corporation (if solo then it's just you)

3. File formal paperwork, usually called "articles of incorporation," and pay a filing fee that ranges from $100 to $800, depending on the state where you incorporate-rate.

4. Create corporate bylaws, which lay out the operating rules for your corporation.

5. Hold the first meeting of the board of directors (not needed if solo)

6. Issue stock certificates to the initial owners (shareholders) of the corporation. (all shares are in your name when solo)

7. Obtain any licenses and permits that are required for your business (as an IC you don't need anything other than your dental license, DEA, malpractice)

Types of Corporations: C vs. S vs. LLC

There are various types of corporations that you can establish each with its pros and cons and specific tax benefits. As dental professionals, we do NOT associate with C corporations, but for completeness of topic, I have included all definitions below.

- C corp applies to large companies with fringe benefits and hundreds of employees. It is a traditional corporation or what we would call "big business providing limited liability to its owners. The company itself is taxed on profits earned by the company. Each of the individual owners files and pays their own income tax on their earnings from salary, dividends, and bonuses. Again, C corps do not apply to us in the dental industry, but knowing this baseline structure will help you differentiate the main two we need to learn below.
- S corp applies to smaller businesses or solo entrepreneurs. It provides the same limited liability as a corporate shareholder but the owner pays taxes as a sole proprietor or partner in a partnership agreement. All business profits "pass-through" to the owners who have the responsibility of reporting them on their personal tax returns. The S Corp itself does not pay income tax but if there is more than one owner, each shareholder must report their portion of the corporate income.
- An LLC or Limited Liability Company a business entity that is separate from its owners. However, unlike a corporation (C or S Corp), an LLC must pay its own taxes. The profits and losses of the business pass through to the owners who are required to report them on their personal tax returns just as they would if they owned a partnership or sole proprietorship. Forming an LLC is less complex and requires less paperwork than a corporation.

Dental associates working as an independent contractor should create either an LLC or S corp for several reasons. Let's look at several characteristics of each type of business.

S corp

- An S corporation generally allows you to pass business losses through to your personal income tax return, where you can use it to offset any income that you accrued from other sources.

- If you decide to sell your S corporation in the future, your taxable gain on the sale of the business can be less than it would have been had you operated the business as a regular corporation.

- S corporation shareholders are not subject to self-employment taxes on the distributions they receive from the corporation (active LLC owners are). These taxes are used to pay your Social Security and Medicare taxes and may equal up to 15% of your income. Since shareholders typically are employed through the corporation, you must pay an employment tax on your employee compensation.

- S corporations are pass-through entities for which shareholders can qualify for the pass-through tax deduction established by the Tax Cuts and Jobs Act. This tax cut makes shareholders eligible to deduct up to 20% of their share of the S corporation's income. However, at some income levels, the deduction is limited to 50% of the W-2 wages the business pays. The fact that the S corporation's owners also typically work as employees of the corporation, can help them qualify for the deduction.

- Aside from the benefits, there are strict restrictions placed on S corporations including the following:
    - Each S corporation shareholder must be a U.S. citizen or resident.
    - S corporations may not have more than 100 shareholders.
    - S corporation profits and losses may be allocated only in proportion to each shareholder's interest in the business.
    - An S corporation shareholder may not deduct corporate losses that exceed his or her "basis" in corporate stock which equals the amount of the shareholder's investment in the company plus or minus a few adjustments.
    - S corporations may not deduct the cost of fringe benefits provided to employee-shareholders who own more than 2% of the corporation.

LLC

Like shareholders of a corporation, all LLC owners are protected from personal liability for business debts and claims.

- An LLC owner can be held personally liable in the eyes of the court if:
    - Personally and directly injure someone
    - Personally guarantee a bank loan or a business debt on which the LLC defaults

- Fails to deposit taxes withheld from employees' wages
- Intentionally does something fraudulent, illegal, or reckless that causes harm to the company or someone else, or
- Treats the LLC as an extension of his or her personal affairs, rather than as a separate legal entity
- If owners don't treat the LLC as a separate business, it can be determined by the legal system that the LLC is not a valid and legitimate business and that its owners are simply individuals who are personally responsible and liable for their actions on behalf of the business. To avoid this, business owners must:
- Act fairly and legally.
- Fund your LLC adequately. Invest enough cash in the business so that your LLC can meet foreseeable expenses and liabilities.
- Maintain separate personal and business expenses.
- Obtain a federal employer identification number (EIN).
- Establish a business-only checking account at a bank.

- For tax purposes, an LLC is considered a "pass-through entity" like a partnership or sole proprietorship. Each owner must report their share of the profits and make quarterly estimated tax payments.

For tax purposes, an LLC is taxed as a sole proprietorship when there is one owner. It is taxed like a general partnership when there are two or more owners. Neither the sole proprietorship nor the general partnership is a taxpaying entity. They are termed "pass-through entities," or conduits. The owners report their share of profit and loss (whether or not it is actually distributed) on their personal income tax returns. You can decide to change the status of your corporation if it benefits you as far as your taxes are concerned after a certain period if your circumstances change or if the structure changes but be sure to consult with an accountant.

For example, there are several types of management structures of an LLC; member management and manager management each having its own unique characteristics. In most small LLCs, member management structure is common in which all members participate equally. Unless you bring on associates and partners to your LLC, as an independent contractor, this structure is suitable.

If you do have multiple owners of an LLC and one member wants to leave, the company must be dissolved and all obligations met. The operating agreement established during incorporation should indicate a "buy-sell" provision to avoid this type of disruption in the management and organization of an LLC.

Steps to form an LLC:

1. File "articles of organization" (in some states called a "certificate of organization" or "certificate of formation") with the Secretary of State.
2. You only need to specify a few basic details about your LLC including name and address, and contact information for a person known as the registered agent who is responsible for filing and maintaining appropriate records for the business.
3. Create a written LLC operating agreement that defines the LLC members' rights and responsibilities, their

percentage interests in the business, and their share of the profits.

4. Apply for a Tax ID number, otherwise known as an EIN, through the Secretary of State where the business will be established. The EIN is to be used instead of your social security number for business transactions.

    ◦ Payroll. If operating as an LLC, you would pay yourself a monthly salary from the business which is then considered a business expense.

    ◦ Health insurance. As a small business, you can elect to provide health insurance through the LLC.

    ◦ Tax benefits. As a business, all business expenses can be deducted from the business tax return including gas, all insurances, business meetings, travel, food, etc. For additional information about what qualifies as a business write off, visit https://www.thebalancesmb.com/. You may be eligible to write off the cost of instruments and a home office.

Note: You must keep documentation as proof of all purchases and expenses in case of an IRS audit for 3 years to justify the expense.

Taxation and Limited Liability are not related

Many small business owners misunderstand the relationship between taxation and limited liability. Because their LLC is treated as a sole proprietorship for tax purposes, they mistakenly believe that liability in the LLC is the same as a liability in these other business types.

Taxation and limited liability are not related at all. Each of the owners of the LLC and corporation enjoys limited liability. In other words, taxation has nothing to do with liability.

Double Taxation

The corporation is considered to be a separate taxpayer in the eyes of the IRS. Taxable income is calculated before shareholders are paid dividends which are taxed at the corporate level. When a corporation does pay a dividend, it is taxable to the owner upon receipt which would cause it to be taxed twice.

Let's take a look at a sample company.

ABC Company has taxable income of $1,000,000 and will pay a $100,000 dividend out of these earnings. If the tax rate is 45 percent, it will pay $450,000 in taxes ($1,000,000 x 45 percent).

If the corporation was able to deduct the dividend, it would have paid only $405,000 in taxes ($900,000 x 45 percent). The shareholder is also responsible to pay tax on the $100,000 received as a dividend.

It is the popular opinion that an LLC offers a tax benefit over a corporation because the "double taxation" of dividends can apply only with a corporation. As the LLC is not a separate, dividend-paying taxpayer, the double taxation concept is not applicable.

Owners can avoid paying dividends in a small corporation by withdrawing cash from the business in other ways such as salary, lease, and loan payments, which will be deductible expenses.

Many small corporations elect subchapter S status as its tax status, thereby not paying income taxes or running into the double taxation issue. This makes double taxation a non-existent problem. That being said, the only real benefit of the LLC over the corporation is in not having to be concerned about double taxation at all.

Pass-Through Tax Deductions and How you Qualify

The Tax Cut and Jobs Act of 2018 allows for owners of a pass-through business to reduce the amount of taxes due. In other words, any business which is not a C corporation receives an additional deduction to level the playing field.

Courtesy of https://www.whitecoatinvestor.com/pass-through-income-deduction/

Home Office

It is important to note in more detail the benefits of a write off for a home office if you are working as an Independent Contractor. Be sure to discuss with your accountant or tax advisor the best way to take advantage of these deductions.

- A home office space is a location within your home that is exclusively used for business purposes and is the same whether you own or rent.
- For 2019, the prescribed rate for eligible tax reduction is $5 per square foot with a maximum of 300 square feet. You may also calculate it as a percentage of space in your home.
- If your home office qualifies for deductions, then you can also deduct some of the overall household costs such as general utilities, homeowner's insurance, general repairs, and maintenance.
- There is a limit on how much you can deduct as business expenses for the business. The home office deductions cannot be more than the business income earned.
- If you include home depreciation as part of the home office deduction and eventually sell your home at a profit, you will have to pay a capital gains tax on the total amount of depreciation deductions you took while you were living there, assuming you sold the home for a profit.

Insurance

As an Independent Contractor and no matter the business type that you have chosen, you have the flexibility to choose the type of insurance plans to participate in. You can be in or out of network independent of the rest of the practice. Even if the practice you work at (or multiple practices) are in-network with a specific insurance plan, you can choose NOT to be a part of that network and therefore not accept the fees of that specific insurance.

However, if your office uses specific insurance and the majority of their patients and income come from those insurance plans, opting to go out of network will significantly reduce the number of patients that will want to have you treat them (as all patients want to have as much covered as possible). While certain procedures may not be covered by insurance, most treatment plans include multiple phases and at least one part of the plan WILL have a potentially covered procedure. Carefully consider your insurance plan options when choosing to operate as an Independent Contractor.

Personal Note:

My own experience followed the lessons above for the independent contractor. For both California and Massachusetts, I created a corporate entity for myself, including articles of incorporation, tax ID number, and all my own insurances including health, disability, and malpractice.

The process was a little bit more of a pain because I had to do it a second time when I moved to Boston. I had to close my corporation in California so as not to be paying for both (unless you plan to live/work bicoastal which is a different story where you will want to have BOTH). But don't EVER consider practicing as an independent contractor here without forming either your own LLC or Corporation. Even if you work as an employee in multiple practices, it may be worth asking your accountant if it's to your benefit to create one as well.

I have an established S-Corp through which I pay myself a salary via a payroll system for my monthly expenses, which I calculated and reviewed with my accountant. The beauty of doing this is that each month I am automatically contributing towards my federal and state taxes, including quarterly estimated tax payments also if necessary. Thus, at year-end, I am not left with a massive tax contribution due, and throughout the year I have a realistic idea of how much money I have in my bank account. It keeps me honest and removes the risk of doing something stupid; there is nothing worse than spending money you think you have but really don't, and suddenly realizing the $50k you may have showing in your account is really more like $15k after your taxes, contributions to savings, etc. It can be deflating, but again it keeps you honest and saves a tremendous amount of hassle.

For my payroll and overall tax work, I use an accounting company that specializes in dental practices. There is a yearly fee associated with the service, but I have found it to be well worth it. That doesn't mean that I'm not on top of my bookkeeping; in fact, I keep track of all my overall expenses and income each month. Believe it or not, for the first several years of my career, I kept track of everything by hand in a written ledger complete with all receipts and paperwork. It made for quite a comical scene at my yearly tax review, but it helped me to better understand all of my expenses and overall financial status. Since then, I just use QuickBooks to do the work for me (much easier this way!), but again I still do all my own balancing.

If you are comfortable doing so, you can plan on doing your own taxes, especially if you are well organized and use QuickBooks. But I still rather save that time for other things.

The insurance process is a pain; there are multiple options for each type and it's difficult to understand the pros and cons for each and how to know what's the best option for you. That's why I've dedicated an entire chapter just for that ahead.

I use my home office as a tax write off along with other expenses such as gas, my car payment, business dinners, conferences, and insurance. As an employee, much of this likely will already be taken care of for you, but it's still to your benefit to educate yourself as much as possible and explore all options. Remember, you may be an employee today, but you may become an owner tomorrow!

PART TWO

Front-end and back-end essentials

4

Protect Yourself; Insurances you must have, and others you could have

"What does 'friends with benefits' even mean?
Does he provide her with health insurance?"
~ Jim Parsons, Big Bang Theory

"Fun is like life insurance; the older you get, the more it costs"
~ Kin Hubbard, American journalist, and humorist

Insurance, insurance, insurance. The list doesn't end. You can get insurance for practically anything but some make more sense than others and there are some you shouldn't live without. Break your arm while skiing? A good health policy can minimize your treatment costs; a good disability policy can help keep you afloat until you can return to work.

Are you the primary source of income for your family? God forbid something tragic or sudden ever happens to you like a car accident or heart attack; what will happen to your family and how they will support themselves moving forward? A good life insurance policy will protect your family for the future.

If you ever needed a lesson in preparing for the unexpected, just look at what's happening now with Covid-19. Things can change in an instant and your career or your life could be jeopardized.

Learn the different options available for each kind of insurance you will need and stay one step ahead.

Necessities for dentists

Malpractice Insurance

Malpractice Insurance, also known more technically as Liability Insurance, is required for a dentist to practice. It protects dental professionals if they are sued for allegedly doing something wrong that resulted in physical harm to the patient. While you may do everything right, each patient is different and may react to drugs and procedures differently. There is always the possibility of complications.

The costs of determining if negligence was a factor when complications occur can result in irreparable damage to a dentist's finances and reputation and temporary or permanent suspension or loss of your license to practice dentistry. Even if the complication is not the dentist's fault, patients can still sue and potentially win. Malpractice insurance protects the dentist and associated assets in the event of this unfortunate situation.

If you are an associate dentist in a practice or an employee, your employer may provide you with Liability Insurance. It is very specific to each office and if you're an independent contractor then you would have to carry your own Liability Insurance. As in all things regarding insurance, it can be very confusing. There are two different kinds of malpractice or liability policies. The policy that will be more applicable to you and your practice depends on which kind of malpractice claims are covered or not covered.

- **Occurrence Made Policy.** In an Occurrence Made Policy, you have coverage for claims that occur while the policy is active. Even if the policy has expired or has been canceled, if the incident happened while the policy was in force then coverage is available. For example, let's say you had policy A from 2014 - 2018 but canceled it in 2019. If in 2020 a claim is brought against you that had occurred in 2017, you will be covered by that policy despite the claim being issued AFTER you canceled it.

- **Claims-Made Policy**. A Claims-Made Policy covers you for claims that occur and are reported while the policy is in force. This last point is extremely important and worth repeating – while in force. In other words, claims must be reported when they occur during the period when coverage is available. Once the policy expires, the coverage expires.

  If your Claims-Made Policy is canceled, you can purchase an extended policy or what's more commonly called **Tail Coverage**. The Tail Coverage extends the time that incidents may be reported. You're probably wondering why would anyone purchase a Claims-Made Policy. The Claims Made Policy is less expensive.

Premiums are lower during the first few years of a Claims-Made Policy and then the rate slowly increases and becomes comparable to the Occurrence Policy rate. Be sure to speak with an insurance agent to determine the best policy for you based on your specialty (general dentist, surgeon, etc.) and of course what you can afford especially when you are first starting.

Important Notice

ACORD **CERTIFICATE OF LIABILITY INSURANCE** DATE (MM/DD/YYYY) 03/26/2012

THIS CERTIFICATE IS ISSUED AS A MATTER OF INFORMATION ONLY AND CONFERS NO RIGHTS UPON THE CERTIFICATE HOLDER. THIS CERTIFICATE DOES NOT AFFIRMATIVELY OR NEGATIVELY AMEND, EXTEND OR ALTER THE COVERAGE AFFORDED BY THE POLICIES BELOW. THIS CERTIFICATE OF INSURANCE DOES NOT CONSTITUTE A CONTRACT BETWEEN THE ISSUING INSURER(S), AUTHORIZED REPRESENTATIVE OR PRODUCER, AND THE CERTIFICATE HOLDER.

IMPORTANT: If the certificate holder is an ADDITIONAL INSURED, the policy(ies) must be endorsed. If SUBROGATION IS WAIVED, subject to the terms and conditions of the policy, certain policies may require an endorsement. A statement on this certificate does not confer rights to the certificate holder in lieu of such endorsement(s).

PRODUCER Phone: (360) 598-3700 Fax: (360) 598-3703
MICHAEL J. HALL & COMPANY
ARCHITECTS & ENGINEERS PROFESSIONAL INSURANCE PROGRAM, INC
19660 10TH AVENUE N.E.
POULSBO WA 98370

CONTACT NAME: MICHAEL J. HALL & COMPANY
PHONE (A/C, No, Ext): (360) 598-3700 FAX (A/C, No): (360) 598-3703
E-MAIL ADDRESS:

Agency Information Provided

INSURED
ABC Corporation
123 Main Street
Anytown, USA 1234-000

INSURER(S) AFFORDING COVERAGE		NAIC #
INSURER A	The Travelers Indemnity Company of America	25666
INSURER B	The Phoenix Insurance Company	25623
INSURER C	The Travelers Indemnity Company	25658
INSURER D	Hartford Casualty Insurance Company	29424
INSURER E		
INSURER F		

COVERAGES CERTIFICATE NUMBER: 156570 REVISION NUMBER:

THIS IS TO CERTIFY THAT THE POLICIES OF INSURANCE LISTED BELOW HAVE BEEN ISSUED TO THE INSURED NAMED ABOVE FOR THE POLICY PERIOD INDICATED. NOTWITHSTANDING ANY REQUIREMENT, TERM OR CONDITION OF ANY CONTRACT OR OTHER DOCUMENT WITH RESPECT TO WHICH THIS CERTIFICATE MAY BE ISSUED OR MAY PERTAIN, THE INSURANCE AFFORDED BY THE POLICIES DESCRIBED HEREIN IS SUBJECT TO ALL THE TERMS, EXCLUSIONS AND CONDITIONS OF SUCH POLICIES. LIMITS SHOWN MAY HAVE BEEN REDUCED BY PAID CLAIMS.

INSR LTR	TYPE OF INSURANCE	ADDL INSR	SUBR WVD	POLICY NUMBER	POLICY EFF (MM/DD/YYYY)	POLICY EXP (MM/DD/YYYY)	LIMITS	
A	GENERAL LIABILITY X COMMERCIAL GENERAL LIABILITY CLAIMS-MADE X OCCUR X XCU / BFPD/ OCP X Separation of Insureds GEN'L AGGREGATE LIMIT APPLIES PER: POLICY X PRO-JECT LOC			680123L456	12/20/11	12/20/12	EACH OCCURRENCE	$ 1,000,000
							DAMAGE TO RENTED PREMISES (Ea occurrence)	$ 300,000
							MED. EXP (Any one person)	$ 5,000
							PERSONAL & ADV INJURY	$ 1,000,000
							GENERAL AGGREGATE	$ 2,000,000
							PRODUCTS - COMP/OP AGG	$ 2,000,000
								$
B	AUTOMOBILE LIABILITY ANY AUTO ALL OWNED AUTOS SCHEDULED AUTOS X HIRED AUTOS X NON-OWNED AUTOS			BA-1234L567	12/20/11	12/20/12	COMBINED SINGLE LIMIT (Ea accident)	$ 1,000,000
							BOD[illegible]URY (Per person)	$
							[illegible] INJURY (Per accident)	$
							[illegible] DAMAGE [illegible]	$
								$
C	X UMBRELLA LIAB X OCCUR EXCESS LIAB CLAIMS-MADE DED X RETENTION $ 10,000			CUP-7941Y21A	12/20[illegible]	12/20/12	EACH OCCURRENCE	$ 5,000,000
							AGGREGATE	$ 5,000,000
								$
D	WORKERS COMPENSATION AND EMPLOYERS' LIABILITY ANY PROPRIETOR/PARTNER/EXECUTIVE OFFICER/MEMBER EXCLUDED? Y/N (Mandatory in NH) If yes, describe under DESCRIPTION OF OPERATIONS below	N/A		52WECTR9085	06/03/11	06/03/12	X WC STATU-TORY LIMITS OTH-ER	$
							E.L. EACH ACCIDENT	$ 1,000,000
							E.L. DISEASE-EA EMPLOYEE	$ 1,000,000
							E.L. DISEASE-POLICY LIMIT	$ 1,000,000
A	Professional Liability:Claims Made Form Pollution Liability: Occurrence Form			[illegible]89	12/20/11	12/20/12	$2,000,000 $2,000,000	

Type of Insurance and Included Coverage

Limits and Coverages

Descriptions of Operations Verbiage

DESCRIPTION OF OPERATIONS / LOCATIONS / VEHICLES [illegible] Remarks Schedule, if more space is required)

Project:

________________ are Additional Insured on the Commercial General Liability and Auto Liability when required by written contract or agreement regarding activities by or on behalf of the Named Insured. This insurance is primary insurance and any other insurance maintained by the Additional Insured shall be excess only and non-contributing with this insurance. A waiver of subrogation applies to the Commercial General Liability, Auto Liability, Umbrella / Excess Liability and Workers Compensation / Employers Liability in favor of the Additional Insured. Additional Insured status is not available on a professional liability policy

CERTIFICATE HOLDER

123 Leasing
456 NE Jefferson Pkwy
Land of Lakes WA 1234-5678

Attention:

CANCELLATION

Cancellation Notice Per Policy Provisions

SHOULD ANY OF THE ABOVE DESCRIBED POLICIES BE CANCELLED BEFORE THE EXPIRATION DATE THEREOF, NOTICE WILL BE DELIVERED IN ACCORDANCE WITH THE POLICY PROVISIONS.

AUTHORIZED REPRESENTATIVE

Signature of Agent

Ashley L. Hurd

ACORD 25 (2010/05)

The limits of coverage of a policy are calculated per claim or in the aggregate or total limit for all claims reported against an insurance policy. For example, the first amount is the amount per claim, and then the second number would be the aggregate or the total limit for all of the claims that can be reported against the insurance policy.

A typical malpractice policy required includes a $1M per patient limit, with a $3 million aggregate, but limits may vary between states and carrier s so do your homework and also inquire with other dentists as to what type of insurance they carry.

There are several ways to reduce the cost of your Malpractice Insurance.

- Receive a discount on your malpractice insurance by taking a risk management course. Of course, you have to take CE courses, but if you can find one that gives risk management credit, it will generally provide a discount on your malpractice policy for up to three years.
- Become a member of a dental organization. The ADA or the EGD provide discounts to their members. Of course, being a member is expensive, but it's something to consider. If the price of being an ADA member for example is too much, at least consider joining your state or local dental society. Oftentimes you can be still eligible for the discount on your insurance.
- Stay free of any claims. If you're claim-free, this helps reduce your insurance costs a lot, and the longer that you remain claim-free, the greater the discount.

Dental Malpractice Insurance is available through a variety of companies including:

- The American Dental Association – most popular
- DentistCare (ProAssurance Group)
- Mitchell & Mitchell Insurance
- Mda Insurance
- MedPro Group (a Berkshire Hathaway company)
- Professional Solutions Insurance Company

Disability Insurance

As you are graduating from dental school and looking at the massive amount of debt that you have accrued, you should be thinking of all the ways where you could save on expenses. However, I can assure you trying to cut out disability insurance is NOT one of them.

According to the American Dental Education Association (ADEA), the "average educational debt for all indebted dental school graduates in the Class of 2016 was $262,119." About 80% of dental grads have student loan debt greater than $100,000, and more than 30% have student loan debt over $300,000."[2]

Fortunately, dentists tend to earn higher incomes faster than in other professions. In other words, they can pay off their loans quicker. According to the Bureau of Labor Statistics, the 2019 median pay for dentists and dental hygienists was $159,200 and $76,220, respectively.[3] For dental specialties, like surgeons and orthodontists, the median pay is more than $200,000.

---

2 https://www.adea.org/GoDental/Money_Matters/Educational_Debt.aspx
3 https://www.bls.gov/ooh/healthcare/dentists.htm

Disability insurance can help to protect both your income and ability to repay this debt if you are injured or unable to work in dentistry. At least 75% of dentists suffer from some sort of a musculoskeletal disorder just because of the way that we work and the demands of our profession. The labor-intensive nature of what we do, leaning over patients all day can lead to chronic back issues, arthritis, knee, and even eyesight and hearing issues. Over time, these demands can wear down your body and you can be more susceptible to injury.

Disability Insurance is probably one of the most confusing types of insurance that we need to purchase as dentists. If you're a practicing dentist, there is a realistic chance that at some point in your career you may have to file a disability claim and therefore, it is highly recommended for all dentists.

It is especially important to buy it when you are younger and while you are healthy. There are even some policies that can be purchased even before you graduate or begin working full-time. However, it's a very confusing topic. There are several different types of Disability Insurance available.

It is equally important to know all the different terminology and definitions for disability insurance, so we have included the most important terms for you below:

Any-occupation versus own-occupation coverage

Any-occupation coverage may afford you lower rates because it is more difficult to qualify for benefits if you become disabled. If you can work in another occupation besides your original one then you are not qualified to receive benefits. However, an Own-occupation policy allows you to receive benefits as long as you demonstrate that you cannot work at your current or most recent occupation.

Attending physician's statement

Underwriting is the process that you go through when you apply for disability insurance and life insurance as well for that matter. The insurer will confirm all the details about your health to ensure validity and usually requires a statement from an attending physician.

Automatic increase benefit

Disability insurance releases benefits to you if you can no longer work as a replacement for the income you would have earned had you not become disabled. An automatic increase benefit is usually offered as a rider in exchange for a higher premier but since it is optional, you may elect to accept the increase or not.

Benefit

Disability benefits are calculated by the number of benefits you would receive when you become disabled and are paid monthly similar to a paycheck. The term in which the benefits are paid may be until you recover or if it is a long-term disability policy, may vary between five years until retirement.

The benefit amount will determine your premium. When calculating it, you should be sure that it will cover 60% to 80% of your pre-tax income before you became disabled. If you pay the premium with pre-tax money, then the benefits received are taxed. Otherwise, they are paid tax-free.

Benefit period

This is the time during which you will receive benefits if you become disabled and is chosen when you first initiate the policy. You may select a shorter benefit period to reduce the premium if a lower premium is desired.

Claim

After you become disabled, you will file a claim to describe the nature of your disability, including when it began and what kind of treatment you've been receiving for it. Most policies require an elimination period so be sure to file as soon as possible after the disability occurs.

Claim form

A claim form is a document on which you will provide all of the information for the insurance company to verify and validate your eligibility to receive benefits.

Cost-of-living adjustment

Increases in the cost of living between the time the policy was issued and the date of the disability will be taken into consideration through a cost-of-living adjustment rider as part of the policy.

Coverage

Coverage is the benefit that you are paying for by taking out the disability insurance policy. The specific details of coverage (what is included and what is not) will be defined in the policy coverage.

Definition of disability

The term disability will be specifically defined by the insurance carrier and may include total, partial, or catastrophic disability. Benefits will be paid according to the severity and duration of the disability. An elimination period may not apply under some definitions of disability, such as presumptive disability.

Elimination period

The elimination period is a waiting period before benefits will be issued once the disability occurs. It can range from between 30 days to 365 days depending on the definition of disability. The elimination period under short-term disability is usually only a few weeks.

The elimination period allows insurance companies to maintain low premiums by allowing policyholders who have become disabled to possibly recover before becoming eligible for benefits.

Exclusion

An activity or exclusion which makes the insured ineligible for benefits should they occur. For most policies, pre-existing conditions are excluded from eligibility.

Future purchase option

As your health declines and up to a certain age, a future purchase option enables you to increase the coverage amount of the policy of course while paying higher premiums.

Group disability insurance

If an employer offers Group disability insurance, it will be a lower cost option as it may be subsidized by the company. On the other hand, the coverage may also be significantly lower than a private disability insurance policy.

Guaranteed renewable

As long as you pay the agreed-upon premium, most disability insurance policies are guaranteed to be renewed with the existing terms.

Long-term disability insurance

Long-term disability insurance (LTDI) offers you the option of receiving benefits for a benefit period that could extend until you retire. Of course, because of the possibility of a longer duration, premiums are commensurate with this possibility.

Medical exam

A medical exam confirms to the insurer that you provided accurate information about your health to the best of your knowledge. Additional medical conditions may be revealed which may exclude or prohibit various types of coverage.

Non-cancelable

As long as you continue to pay the premium, the disability insurance company cannot increase your premium. It may be included at an additional cost on your premium as a rider to the policy.

Overinsurance

It is possible to purchase more insurance than you need. While many people estimate their benefits based on 60 – 80% of their pre-tax income, some may overestimate and have more coverage than needed in the event that they suffer a disability.

Own-occupation

Own-occupation describes disability insurance that covers if you are too injured or ill to continue in your current line of work but may be able to work in another occupation. Under this type of policy coverage, if you can still do function in another line of work, you may be eligible for benefits.

Policy

The policy is a document that clearly defines the various definitions of disability, the conditions of benefit eligibility, any applicable exclusions, premium, benefit amount, and the benefit period. It is a binding agreement between you and the disability insurance company.

Pre-existing condition

Any medical issue that you had before taking out the disability insurance policy is considered to be a pre-existing condition. Many pre-existing conditions are excluded from coverage and will not be eligible for disability benefits.

Premium

The amount that you pay to the insurance company each month based on the policy agreement is called the premium. The rate is pre-determined based on the coverage you select, benefit amount, benefit period, and any pre-existing conditions. On average premium prices range between 1% and 3% of your income.

Reconsideration period

If you are disabled by something that is considered as an exclusion on your disability policy, you can still request that your claim and benefits be approved. The reconsideration period which is included in some insurance policy riders allows you to ask the insurance company to consider removing the exclusion and allowing your disability to be covered.

Rider

In addition to the definitions included in the policy, there may be additional terms and conditions included in another document called a rider. Typically, a rider will enhance the coverage of the policy and may include conditions of eligibility that may not have been defined in the policy.

Short-term disability insurance

Short-term disability insurance (STDI) is meant to provide coverage for a short period while you are recovering. It has a short elimination period and benefits are usually distributed for several months up to one year.

Simplified issue

There is a way of determining premiums without having to undergo a medical exam which is called simplified issue. Coverage is available faster but the benefit amount may be lower than a traditional disability insurance policy and certain exclusions may apply.

Social Security disability insurance

Social Security disability insurance (SSDI) may be an option for anyone who cannot afford a private policy. The Social Security Administration's definition of disability is much less lenient than a typical disability insurance plan with many exclusions and smaller disability benefits.

Survivor benefit

If you are to pass away while receiving disability benefits, some policies allow for a beneficiary to be designated and to receive the equivalent of a few months' worth of your coverage. It is not the most beneficial type of policy to help cover incurred expenses and a life insurance policy may be more appropriate.

Underinsurance

Just as you can have too much insurance, you can also be underinsured or have less coverage than you need. To pay a lower premium, some may underestimate their coverage needs. If you become disabled and need to rely on disability coverage, you may find yourself in a difficult position.

Underwriting

After you have applied for disability insurance, an underwriter reviews your medical records, medical history, finances, tax returns, bank statements in a process called underwriting. They will then determine your eligibility and premium rate.

A disability insurance policy should also include occupation class, beginning (elimination) date, total and partial disability benefits, and the benefit period. When you begin your search for an insurance provider to purchase your policy from, be sure to research the reputation of the company with others who have worked with them including their history on paying claims and premium rates.

Occupation Class

To properly assess the amount of risk involved when offering long-term disability insurance coverage, companies have created occupational classes based on associated hazards and risks of the job. Occupations are generally classified on a scale between 1 to 6, with 1 being the highest risk and therefore, highest premiums. The classes also act as a guide as to what can and cannot be paid on a claim as well as the allowable benefits.

Typically, medical professionals are designated with an M and fall into varying classes depending upon the specialty. For example, family physicians and internists are in a higher class and therefore, should expect lower insurance premiums. Conversely, emergency room physicians and surgeons are considered higher risk and therefore will pay higher premiums. Depending upon the insurance carrier, they typically classify dentistry in the 3 – 4 range when it comes to risk according to the 2020 rates of most providers. Be sure to assess your occupation class when selecting an insurance provider to obtain the best and most appropriate benefits for you.

Employer-Sponsored Disability Insurance

Employer-Sponsored Disability Insurance is something you would typically find if you work for a corporate dental office and part of your benefits are based on a percentage of your salary. You would lose that insurance if you change jobs. If you work for multiple employers, then this is a less attractive option. If you are planning on having your own practice and/or being self-employed, then this is also not the way to go.

Group Disability Insurance

Group Disability Insurance is made available to Members of organizations such as the American Dental Association or similar groups. Members typically are covered until age 67 as true own occupation and will cover both partial and full disability, with income replacement up to $180,000 a year. Thus, while offering good benefits, your policy is not under your control and is owned by the group itself, which means they can negotiate or renegotiate the terms at any time on their own. You would still get a monthly benefit based on the percentage of your base salary, but the control is not in your hands.

Individual Disability Insurance

Individual Disability Insurance is the most common kind of disability insurance. An Individual policy is going to be the best choice for most dentists because they're more favorable. There are generally speaking three different types of individual disability definitions you should know: Any, Own, and Modified.

As explained earlier, an any-occupation policy will pay benefits if you are unable to work in ANY occupation. An own-occupation policy will pay benefits if you are unable to perform the duties of your current position. You can be employed in an alternate occupation and still receive benefits against your policy. We have not yet touched on the modified policy which permits you to work in another occupation but with restrictions. The amount of the benefit paid in the other profession will be subtracted from the total benefits paid. In the dental profession, you will want to purchase an own-occupation policy.

Be sure to carefully review your individual policy. For example, many policies contain a No Work provision that precludes them from receiving disability benefits even if they're working in any capacity, meaning not even working in dentistry. Make sure that there's not a No Work provision in your policy.

The second thing to look for in your disability policy is to make sure you have enough coverage. Many of us sign up for our first disability policy when we graduate dental school or shortly after we start a practice. We don't really think about it much until the time comes to potentially file a claim. Then we realize that the monthly benefit is less than the income that we're actually making. You want to make sure that you adjust your disability coverage to reflect your current financial circumstances as your circumstances change throughout your career.

Payment Options

When it comes to receiving Disability payments, you have several choices: graded payments or level payments. It is important to understand the differences between each and your choices when purchasing long-term disability insurance.

Consider how you would like to protect your income:

a. Pay higher premiums but maintain this throughout the life of the policy

   or

b. Pay lower premiums in the early part of the policy life and pay more as time goes on

Level Premium Payments

If you have a non-cancelable and/or guaranteed renewable policy, your premium payment will stay the same or level for as long as you continue to make payments on the policy. The premium is typically higher to ensure that the insurance company is guaranteed to receive their benefit should you file a claim relatively early in the term of the policy.

Graded Premium Payments

Conversely, a graded premium payment begins at a lower payment amount and gradually increases over the length of the policy term typically every year. As time goes on, you are more likely to file a claim.

Which premium structure is better?

If you can afford the higher premium, at least you know that this rate will never increase. Although it may be difficult at the onset, you know that your income will increase and while other expenses will also rise, you can be assured that your disability insurance payment will not ever change.

If you are purchasing your disability insurance policy while still a student or when you first begin your practice, it may be more advantageous to have a graded premium payment with its lower rate. You still have the benefit of the same insurance coverage while paying a lower premium at a time when it may be most difficult.

The difference between level and graded premium structure may be as significant as 40% so carefully consider which option will be right for you.

Duration of policy

If you believe that you may drop the insurance coverage, a graded premium is a better option than the level payment option. Assuming that you purchase a policy in your 20's, financial experts believe that the break-even point is in your early 50s at which time you will then be paying more for the graded premium than the level premium.

In general, most insurance companies will allow you to make a change from a graded premium plan to a level plan on the anniversary of policy issue. That being said, you may elect to begin with a graded premium and after several years when your income has increased to switch to the level payment option. However, keep in mind that the level premium will be determined by your age at the time of the switch.

How can you increase your disability coverage?

Some companies offer automatic increase riders which periodically automatically increase your benefit over time as long as you've agreed to pay a higher premium with each benefit increase. As you age and the profession begins to take a toll on your body, you must increase the disability benefit based on your current income. Another option is called a Future Increase Option Rider which allows you to purchase additional coverage without changing the terms of your existing policy.

Whenever you are trying to qualify for an increase in your benefits, you will have to disclose new financial information, but depending on the policy you won't have to go through a new update to your medical status. This is very important because as we grow older, we're probably going to have new medical conditions or diagnoses that we did not have when we first purchased our Disability Insurance and those new conditions could potentially prevent us from being eligible for additional coverage. Keep in mind most policies only allow for benefit increases during certain times set forth by the policy typically when the policy is about to expire or its anniversary date. The verification process is necessary because you cannot claim more in benefits than you earn.

It is important to carefully read your policy to make sure that you don't miss out on the option to increase your coverage. In case the policy that you have doesn't have an increase option, you can purchase a separate policy with a different carrier to increase your total monthly benefit. However, if you're going to purchase an additional Disability Insurance, be sure that they complement one another rather than cancel each other out. For example, many policies have provisions known as "Work provisions" which require the policyholder to work in some capacity to be eligible to collect benefits. But if you have a second policy that includes a No-Work provision, then it would be impossible to collect the full benefit as one would negate the other.

The income portion of this discussion is so important that it is worth repeating. The more that you earn, the more coverage that you can purchase. Another way of looking at it is that disability insurance will pay relative to your loss of earnings. As you earn a higher income, you want to be sure that you are compensated accordingly for it during a time when you can no longer earn it, temporarily or permanently. Therefore, as you grow in your profession over the years, you will want to purchase more coverage.

For those readers who are still currently in dental school, be aware that you can apply for a policy even as a student and receive coverage in case anything happens during your four years. This coverage can then carry on with you after graduation and build up from there.

Let's look at some other terms of disability insurance policies.

- Waiting periods for coverage can be 30, 60, 90 days, etc. The longer the waiting period, the lower the premium.
- The length of your coverage is referred to as the Benefit Period. The typical benefit period goes up to the age of 65 to 67 and then to 70. The longer the benefit period, the higher the cost.
- Short-term versus long-term disability insurance.
    - Short-Term Disability Insurance (STDI) replaces your income for three to six months if you experience an injury or illness and typically covers up to 80% of your income while you are unable to work. STDI has a waiting period of typically 14 days after processing before you begin receiving benefits. The cost of this type of policy is dependent upon income (therefore

coverage amount), occupation, age, gender, health, and benefit and elimination period.

- Long-Term Disability Insurance (LTDI) replaces your income for a longer-term depending on the benefit period that you choose. It is important to note that the benefit period selected will increase the premium accordingly. For example, if you want a 10-year benefit if you are sick or injured, the policy premium will be significantly higher than a two or three-year benefit period. Short-term disability benefits would apply before long-term benefits kick in.

- Riders for policy. Riders come with an additional cost to your policy. One of the most important riders that you can purchase as a dentist is called the Own Occupation Rider. It allows you to still receive your full disability benefit if you are disabled. The coverage will not be reduced if you return to work in another occupation. For example, let's say you get into a car accident and you are unable to practice dentistry. With the Own Occupation Rider, the insurance company won't reduce your Disability Insurance benefits if you return to work in a different profession. However, it will need to be proven through the claims process that you truly are incapable of practicing dentistry to be covered. According to my financial advisor, the percentage of these types of successful claims is low.

- Partial Disability Rider. A Partial Disability Rider is potentially very useful if you suffer a disability in which you're still able to practice, but you suffer a loss of income due to the disability. For example, if you have a back problem that forces you to practice on a more limited basis, you are going to lose income. Due to this loss of income, you may then be eligible for partial or residual disability benefits. This would also apply if a person was diagnosed with a serious health condition that required them to take extended time off work or cut back hours due to undergoing treatment.

Most companies require a minimum threshold of loss of income to be able to qualify for partial disability benefits, usually around 15 to 20 percent of the loss.

- Student loan rider. You can purchase this additional rider to guarantee that your student loan is paid if you are unable to work. Of course, this does increase your premium so keep in that in mind when considering the overall cost of your disability policy.
- Many other types of riders are available and disability insurance can be very complex. The important thing is to speak with a qualified, experienced insurance agent and read your policy very carefully. The following are several recommended insurance companies offering the best disability insurance options for dentists:
    - Ameritas
    - MedPro
    - Assurity
    - Guardian-Berkshire
    - Principal
    - The Standard
    - MassMutual
    - Mutual of Omaha

LONG TERM DISABILITY CLAIM FORM EMPLOYEE STATEMENT

MetLife
Metropolitan Life Insurance Company
P.O. Box 14590
Lexington, KY 40511
Fax: 1-800-230-9531

Instructions for completing the claim form:
1. Complete all applicable areas of the claim form.
2. If you are the Authorized Representative, include a copy of the legal document(s) authorizing you to act on the Employee/Claimant's behalf.
3. Sign the claim form.
4. Fax this form to expedite your claim – retain original for your records.
5. *Contact MetLife at 888-444-1433 for any questions you have on completing this form.

Section 1: Personal Information

Name (Last, First, MI) – MUST ANSWER	Employer – MUST ANSWER	Group Report #	ID Number

Address	City	State	Zip Code	Date of Birth (MM/DD/YY) mm/dd/yy	Sex ☐M ☐F	Social Security # MUST ANSWER

Home Phone #	Work Phone #	Occupation	Marital Status ☐ Married ☐ Single ☐ Other	Tax Exemptions

Dependent Information:

	Name	Date of Birth	SS#
Spouse		mm/dd/yy	
Children		mm/dd/yy	
		mm/dd/yy	
		mm/dd/yy	

Section 2: Claim Information

Is your disability due to ☐ Injury/Accident? ☐ Illness? | If due to injury/accident, give date, time and details.

Is this condition work related? ☐ Yes ☐ No | (When, Where, How)

Date of first treatment for this condition mm/dd/yy	**Date Last Worked** MUST ANSWER mm/dd/yy	Date Disability Began mm/dd/yy	Height	Weight

Name, address, phone number of your primary attending physician.

Name of physicians/providers who have treated you within the past 2 years.

Name of Physician/Provider	Phone Number	Dates of Treatment	Reason for Visit
		From mm/dd/yy To mm/dd/yy	
		From mm/dd/yy To mm/dd/yy	
		From mm/dd/yy To mm/dd/yy	

Has the patient been hospitalized? ☐ Yes ☐ No If Yes, give dates from mm/dd/yy to mm/dd/yy ☐ Inpatient ☐ Outpatient
Name and address of hospital

Circle Highest Education Level Completed.
1 2 3 4 5 6 7 8 9 10 11 12 13 14 15 16 17 18
| Degrees, Certificates, License/Skills or training obtained

Please describe what prevents you from performing the duties of your job.

Have you applied for or are you receiving income from any other sources? ☐ Yes ☐ No
If yes, provide the following information.

	Applied for	Receiving	$ Amount	Frequency	From/To Dates
Salary Continuance/Sick Leave	☐	☐			mm/dd/yy mm/dd/yy
Short Term Disability	☐	☐			mm/dd/yy mm/dd/yy
Worker's Compensation	☐	☐			mm/dd/yy mm/dd/yy
State Disability	☐	☐			mm/dd/yy mm/dd/yy
Social Security	☐	☐			mm/dd/yy mm/dd/yy
Dependent Social Security	☐	☐			mm/dd/yy mm/dd/yy
No Fault (Income Replacement)	☐	☐			mm/dd/yy mm/dd/yy
Retirement/Pension	☐	☐			mm/dd/yy mm/dd/yy
Permanent Total Disability	☐	☐			mm/dd/yy mm/dd/yy
Other (Please Identify)	☐	☐			mm/dd/yy mm/dd/yy

Page 1 of 5
EES LTD 5323 (06/14) Fs

According to a friend in the industry and personal financial advisor, when considering which company to use for disability insurance, it is recommended through personal experience to use a mutual company versus a stock company. Because a mutual company's policyholders are in fact shareholders in the company, there is a vested interest in managing the plans well and therefore, should give you peace of mind that your money and future are secure.

Health Insurance

Health insurance is designed to provide financial coverage for medical costs. If you own a practice, this is a benefit that you should consider not only for yourself and your family but if you want to offer it as a benefit for your employees. As a dental associate, consider whether the practice offers health insurance before signing on the dotted line as discussed earlier.

If you are an independent contractor, you can purchase individual health insurance through the government or your state's exchange. However, it is important to note that premiums will be higher for an individual versus a group plan (as offered through many practices).

To be sure that you get the most of out your health insurance, it is important to understand the two basic types: individual versus group health insurance.

Individual Health Insurance Plan

- Typically purchased for a single person or family when not offered as part of an employment package from a dental practice. It is typically available through a healthcare exchange or a private insurance company.
- The premiums are typically higher and this type of insurance is not accepted by all medical practitioners.

- It is portable and not dependent upon your employer and therefore is the logical choice for independent contractors or those who work for multiple offices.
- As the owner of a practice, you may consider this type of insurance if you are just starting out and have no employees.

Group Health Insurance Plan

- Purchased for a group of members typically by an employer for the employees.
- Risk is shared across the plan and therefore, the premiums are typically less per person or family.
- Because the plan is considered a benefit of working for an employer, it is not portable and will usually end when you no longer work for the practice.
- As a practice owner, you must consider the cost of health insurance benefits. Employees pay their own premiums through payroll deductions but you as the employer are still responsible for submitting payment to the health insurance provider every month. Depending upon the number of employees that you have, this can be a hefty number.
- Per the Affordable Care Act, pre-existing conditions and income do not play a factor in healthcare premiums. Instead, age and the type of plan selected are the only factors used to determine premium costs.
- While there are many benefits to offering group health insurance, one major benefit to employees is that employees will pay for their premiums through payroll deductions using Pre-tax dollars, reducing the overall amount that they pay in premiums.

General Liability Coverage

Like all businesses, dentists are required to have General Liability Insurance to protect them from unexpected events that may occur such as a slip and fall in the office or damage to a patient's prepaid dentures.

General Liability Insurance is available from your insurance agent. Be sure to discuss the options and terms before buying any policy as the benefits and plans may vary depending upon your location, risk assessment, size of the office, and the number of employees.

Property Insurance

Property insurance covers the repair or replacement of all of the contents of your office including the structure, furniture, computers, supplies, and equipment in the event of unforeseen circumstances such as vandalism, fire, hail storms, etc. This insurance is available through your insurance agent and is necessary to guarantee to protect you from financial ruin in the event of a catastrophic event or situation.

Equipment Insurance

As a dentist, your ability to work depends on the reliability of your office's sophisticated equipment including dental vacuum systems, cabinet-mounted X-ray machines, computer imaging systems, tools, etc. You can purchase specialized equipment insurance typically through the same insurance agent who provides your liability insurance to help pay for repairs to the tools of the trade if they malfunction.

It may also help to replace the lost income and other expenses related to equipment breakdowns and delays. Most policies include a deductible and payout limit for this type of coverage.

Data Compromise Insurance

In today's highly digital world, everything including patient records including personal, medical, and financial information is maintained electronically. Unfortunately, this also leaves practices exposed and vulnerable to cyber-attacks and possibly identity theft. In addition to having a robust data-security system in place, you may consider purchasing Data Compromise Insurance if your practice is the victim of such an attack.

Life Insurance

Life insurance helps provide peace of mind that your family will be taken care of after you are gone by providing tax-free money to your loved ones when you die.

You are working hard to create a life for yourself and your loved ones. You should also be sure to protect your hard-earned assets and to leave a legacy for your children or to provide a benefit to others.

While you may just be coming out of school and not thinking about life insurance as a priority, there are good reasons to start young. Since most policies are age-based, the premium due for a term or permanent life insurance policy for someone in their twenties is going to be significantly lower than a person in their thirties or forties. Most people think that since they do not have a spouse, children, or even any assets yet, that they do not have to have life insurance.

However, once they decide to purchase it at a much older age, the premiums are significantly higher and benefits may be less. My advice to you is to buy life insurance NOW when it is fairly inexpensive. For example, as a healthy young adult in your later twenties or early thirties, you could purchase a $500,000 term life insurance policy for $15 or $20 per month. That's definitely a much more manageable number than one would expect!

There are two types of life insurance each with important differences:

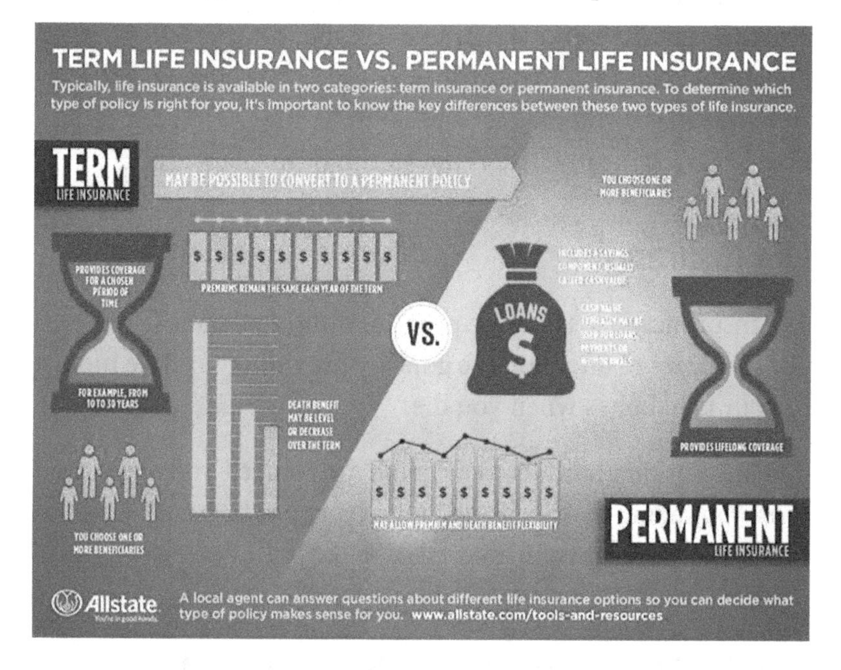

Term Life Insurance

- A term life insurance policy is established for a specific number of years, typically 20 – 30 years but can be renewed upon expiration.
- It provides tax-free money to the beneficiaries of the policy upon your death.

- Term life insurance premiums are generally less expensive than permanent insurance premiums.
- It may be converted upon policy expiration to a permanent policy.

Permanent Life Insurance

- The policy remains in effect for as long as you continue paying the premium.
- Offers various options:
    - Whole Life – Pay a fixed premium and receive a fixed death benefit. The policy accumulates a cash value.
    - Universal Life – The premium amount can change and therefore the death benefit along with it. The policy typically accumulates a cash value. Interest is applied at a fixed rate.
    - Indexed Universal Life – Similar to Universal Life, this type of policy is different in the way interest is credited to the cash value of the policy. Interest is applied based on stock market indexes.
    - Variable Universal Life – Combines the flexible premium option of universal life but the interest is tied to the performance of investment accounts.

Everyone should have a personal life insurance policy even to cover death benefits and basic needs. You may consider a permanent policy as a retirement savings account that can grow tax-deferred to be used at a later time. No matter the type of life insurance policy that you elect to purchase, there are several key factors to keep in mind:

- Duration of term. Consider whether you want coverage for a specific period or if you want the additional benefit of accumulating cash value.
- Cost. Term Life Insurance policies come with a significantly reduced premium cost. Also, it is important to note that age plays a factor in the cost of the policy so again it's advisable to consider purchasing either type of plan when you are young. Most term policies can be converted to permanent policies later in the term. This may be an IDEAL option to balance initial financial needs with your more secure financial position later in your career.
- Permanent policies provide the added benefit of having a cash value. Your tolerance to risk should be considered as a factor when evaluating policy types. Do you want to bear the risk of the market as it fluctuates or are you more comfortable with a fixed rate of interest? This is a personal preference.

To purchase a life insurance policy, whether a term or permanent policy, you will be required to complete a medical questionnaire and more than likely have a physical. Since premiums are directly connected to age, this is yet another reason you should consider purchasing a plan when you are young and while you are healthy.

Begin the process of purchasing a life insurance policy by contacting a financial advisor. They can steer you in the right direction based on your current age, income, and overall status.

			Policy 1 Designed for Maximum Death Benefit		Policy 2 Designed for Accelerated Cash Value Growth		Policy 3 Designed for Maximum Cash Value Growth	
			All Base		Base + Paid Up Additions		Base + Paid Up Additions + Term	
Policy Year	Age	Net Annual Premium	Annual Cash Value Increase*	Total Cash Value*	Annual Cash Value Increase*	Total Cash Value*	Annual Cash Value Increase*	Total Cash Value*
1	**36**	$12,000	$1,107	$1,107	$6,745	$6,745	$8,495	$8,495
4	**39**	$12,000	$10,070	$29,098	$11,869	$40,360	$12,337	$43,608
5	**40**	$12,000	$10,855	$39,953	$12,572	$52,932	$13,007	$56,616
7	**42**	$12,000	$12,405	$64,004	$14,016	$80,241	$14,404	$84,719
10	**45**	$12,000	$14,721	$105,912	$16,287	$126,826	$16,748	$132,688
15	**50**	$12,000	$19,191	$193,314	$20,741	$221,570	$21,183	$229,535
20	**55**	$12,000	$23,048	$301,009	$25,390	$339,131	$26,077	$349,956
25	**60**	$12,000	$26,432	$424,647	$30,366	$479,907	$31,558	$495,901
30	**65**	$12,000	$30,903	$570,082	$36,331	$649,384	$37,994	$672,718
40	**75**	$12,000	$42,490	$940,366	$51,546	$1,093,442	$54,351	$1,139,545
50	**85**	$0	$49,038	$1,377,040	$57,021	$1,601,199	$59,425	$1,668,710
60	**95**	$0	$59,917	$1,926,446	$69,671	$2,240,039	$72,608	$2,334,486

Table A: Cash Values in three dividend-paying whole life policies on a male, age 35, in good health

---

Personal Note:

Just to give you some perspective on how I have handled the various insurance requirements, I have given you my current insurance carriers below.

Malpractice – MedPro. They do it all, including disability and financial services. I started with TDIC in California, and then EDIC when I moved back to Boston. My EDIC policy was linked to being a member of the Massachusetts Dental Society; good business for them, but I don't like being tied up by one company to another. My experience with EDIC was fantastic and I think they are top-notch…but MedPro has been equally good since.

Disability - Guardian and MedPro. Yes, you can have more than one carrier and policy. Get as much as you can so you can be covered if an accident disables you from practicing. With Guardian, I was able to get a policy without the no-work provision; so, I can continue working in a different capacity and still keep my policy if it was determined that I have a legitimate complete disability (like teaching full-time for example). I added MedPro a few years ago to add additional coverage as I had maxed out with Guardian for the year. Just recently during the writing of this book, I was able to again raise my total coverage via Guardian an additional $2500/month. It's definitely worth the investment as every dollar will count in a worst-case scenario!

Health Insurance - Currently I have Tufts Health. There are too many options out there, some with better coverage than others. Most people without pre-existing conditions start with a simpler plan after school since you are younger and typically healthier to save on the premium, but this again varies for everyone. Regardless of the carrier, health insurance is one insurance you cannot, and should not, live without. Premiums can cost significantly more if you are married, have kids, etc as more people are being covered.

Even as a single individual, your policy will likely slowly increase in rate each year. If you are young and healthy, you can always start with a cheaper policy with less coverage to save money early in your career. If anything was to occur, you are always able to up your policy as well. It's always tempting to try and ignore purchasing this insurance for some who are healthy (I have known a friend who didn't purchase for several years after residency), but your health is one area I would never gamble with.

Life insurance - I recently began funding a permanent "whole life" term policy. It's a long-term investment for me, slowly builds with time, yet I can access funds at any time if needed in case of an emergency. It's a good combination of investment and savings, but it depends on your situation and whether you have a spouse and/or children which I don't yet. Speak with your advisor and do your due diligence to determine what is the best option for you.

The bottom line of this chapter is that when it comes to insurance, you have to be prepared. You must have a plan to account for the unexpected (or in the case of disability, maybe the expected). It is never too early to be concerned about life insurance even as you are just starting out in life. It will be too late to think about these things when and if you need it or as you get ready to retire. Again, you can purchase some of these various types of insurance even while you are still in dental school. Don't delay!

5

Savings and Retirement; Preparing for the end from Day 1

"Greed is good"
~ Gordon Gecko - Wall Street

"Strategy without tactics is the slowest route to victory. Tactics without strategy is the noise before defeat."
~ Sun Tzu - The Art of War

I am typing away here in week 3 of my unemployment. Massachusetts is rightfully taking an aggressive approach to dealing with the coronavirus pandemic which means outside of some walks with the pup, I am spending some serious time at home.

If you would have told me, or anyone in the world, a month ago that the world would essentially shut down for an indefinite period, I would never believe you. Alas, here we are, and even with the reassuring economic loans being offered by the government, dentists are concerned. Not only are we at high risk once we return to work, but financially this has put a massive strain on owners and employees alike. If you didn't have some money stored away for a rainy day, then you are certainly at risk of being swept away by the storm.

That's why you must prepare for a worst-case scenario from day 1. Of course, pandemics aside, even in ideal times you want to be planning for your retirement. Setting aside some of your income each month for savings, investments, or a backup fund is an essential step to assuring you have a comfortable life to look forward to once you retire, not to mention in case of any short term or indefinite emergency. You always want an extra chair lying around in case the music ever stops.

How much do you need to set aside each month to live comfortably once you call it quits? Let's review some of your options; you may be surprised to find that you need to save a whole lot more than you imagined.

The Silent Killer: Beware of Fees

"Trust, but verify"
~ Ronald Reagan - POTUS 1980 - 1988

Financial advisors are there to advise, but many are advising on behalf of themselves and their company (self-interest) as much as yours. How can that be though? You are giving them your own money; they are promising great returns and showing you all sorts of graphs and charts that imply you will be sitting pretty by the time you want to retire. Sounds like you are in good hands.

Flashback spring 2013

In my past life, before dental school, I was a political science major. I was debating between a career in foreign service or follow my older sister's footsteps and become a dentist. Well, you know how that ended.

Anyways, I still keep up with current events and my favorite documentary series has always been PBS FRONTLINE. No BS, no political bias, just good investigative reporting. Oftentimes, the news says one thing about a policy and then when they have an interview with the person who drafted the same policy him/herself, they say something very different. Watching their programs makes me happy that I chose dental school in many ways!

One program they had was a massive eye-opener for me and I would highly suggest each of you finding an hour one night after dinner to watch. The episode is called "The Retirement Gamble". Its lessons may save you tens of thousands, if not nearly your entire future retirement account.

Retirement Planning

Most financial experts advise saving 20% of your after-tax income per month. This is understandably difficult and terrifying at the same time as you consider that you have recently graduated, may not have a job yet, and those student loans looming over your head. It will require a budget and a lot of discipline.

As a young professional, it is important to start saving for your future as soon as possible. Develop a consistent strategy and habits that are geared toward long-term objectives to complement your short-term goals. What does this mean? That means while you are building your life, saving to purchase a car or a home in the short-term, and building your business, you must also be consistently putting money aside for retirement as well.

This certainly sounds complicated so let's break it down. There are two very popular approaches to savings for the general population.

The 50/30/20 Rule

First, let's look at the ever-popular 50/30/20 budget rule. Senator Elizabeth Warren introduced the rule in the book, *All Your Worth: The Ultimate Lifetime Money Plan*, which she co-authored with her daughter. Instead of trying to follow a complicated, crazy-number-of-lines budget, you can think of your money as sitting in three buckets.

- Costs that Don't Change (Fixed): 50%

  It would be nice if you didn't have those regular monthly bills such as the electric bill, water, phone, car, and mortgage (or rent) bills. And don't forget about those student loans.

- Discretionary Money: 30%

  This is the bucket where anything (within reason) goes. It's your money to use on wants instead of needs. Most people include food in this bucket although it is a necessity since you do have options such as buying groceries, eating out, or ordering in.

  You would also include entertainment such as date night and movies and miscellaneous purchases in the discretionary fund since these are not necessarily things that you need (date night, buying a new television, and charitable contributions). Many financial advisors argue that 30% in a discretionary bucket is too high and some of these funds should be transferred to savings.

- Financial Goals: 20%

  If you're not aggressively saving for the future—by funding an IRA, a 529 plan if you have kids, and, of course, contributing to a 401(k) or another retirement plan, you're setting yourself up for hard times ahead. This funding is essential for your future. Retirement funds like IRAs and Roth IRAs can be set up through most brokerages.

  If you don't have an emergency fund, most of this 20% should go first to creating one.

The 50/30/20 Budget Rule

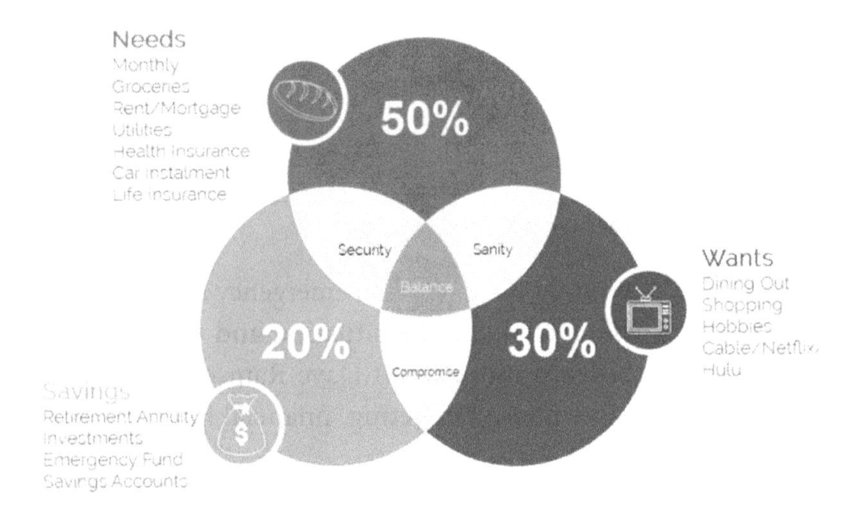

Dave Ramsey

Financial guru Dave Ramsey has a different take on how you should carve up your cash. His recommended allocations look something like this (expressed as a percentage of your take-home pay):

- Charitable Giving: 10%
- Savings: 10%
- Food: 10%–15%
- Utilities: 5%–10%
- Housing: 25%
- Transportation: 10%
- Medical/Health: 5%–10%
- Insurance: 10%–25%
- Recreation: 5%–10%
- Personal Spending: 5%–10%
- Miscellaneous: 5%–10

How much cash you should keep in an emergency fund depends largely on your financial and life situation and your savings goals. Be sure to learn more about Dave Ramsey's Financial Peace to learn more about budgeting, financial management, and investing.

Retirement Planning Options: Where to Invest your Savings

There are many types of investment options available and to a novice, they are overwhelming and confusing. Let's look at several of the many plans and opportunities for you to begin saving for your retirement.

If you are just starting out, retirement may be the very last thing on your mind but in fact, it should be the first thing. There is no time like the present to begin saving for tomorrow. Although it may seem difficult at the moment, you will thank yourself later.

What is a 401(k) Plan?

A 401(k) plan is a tax-advantaged defined-contribution retirement account. This can be any type of investment, financial account, or savings plan that is either exempt from taxation, tax-deferred, or that offers other types of tax benefits.

Employees can make contributions to their 401(k) accounts through automatic payroll withholding, and employers can match some or all of those contributions depending upon the type of plan. Investment earnings in a traditional 401(k) plan are not taxed until the employee withdraws that money, typically after retirement. In a Roth 401(k) plan, withdrawals are tax-free since contributions are made pre-tax.

Participants should remember that once their money is in a 401(k), either a traditional or Roth IRA, it may be difficult to withdraw it without penalty.

IRA Plans

- Roth, traditional, and SEP IRAs can serve different purposes for different people. To determine the best option for you, be sure to reach out to your financial advisor for advice and guidance.
- A traditional IRA offers an upfront tax break, while with a Roth your tax break occurs in the future.
- If you are self-employed, a SEP IRA will allow you to save more for retirement than either a traditional IRA or a Roth.

Traditional IRAs

A traditional IRA allows you to contribute on a pre-tax basis into the investments of your choice, which will then grow tax-deferred until you eventually withdraw the money. You have the option of rolling funds from other 401 K plans into a traditional IRA. For example, if you were offered and contributed to a 401K at a previous employer, you can roll those funds together into a Traditional IRA account.

Provided that your income is below specific limits and you meet other requirements (such as not having another eligible workplace retirement plan), you can take a tax deduction for your contributions to a traditional IRA. When you withdraw money from this type of account in retirement, those funds will be taxed as ordinary income. According to the IRS, you must begin to take **Required Minimum Distributions** (RMD) from the account each year after you turn 72.

As of 2020, remaining the same from 2019, the traditional IRA contribution limit is set at $6,000 a year, with the option of an additional $1,000 catch-up contribution if you're 50 or older, for a total of $7,000.

If you do not work in an environment that offers access to a retirement plan, and/or if you think you'll be in a lower tax bracket after you retire, then a traditional IRA may be your preferred method of saving for retirement since funds will be taxed at the rate at which you qualify for at the time.

Roth IRA

The Roth IRA, introduced in 1997, functions very much like a traditional IRA but in reverse.

While the contribution limits are the same for both Roth and traditional IRAs, including catch-up contributions, there are no upfront tax deductions associated with a Roth IRA. When the money is withdrawn, you will not be charged tax. For professionals who believe that they will be in a higher tax bracket after retirement, contributing funds to a Roth IRA is the better option.

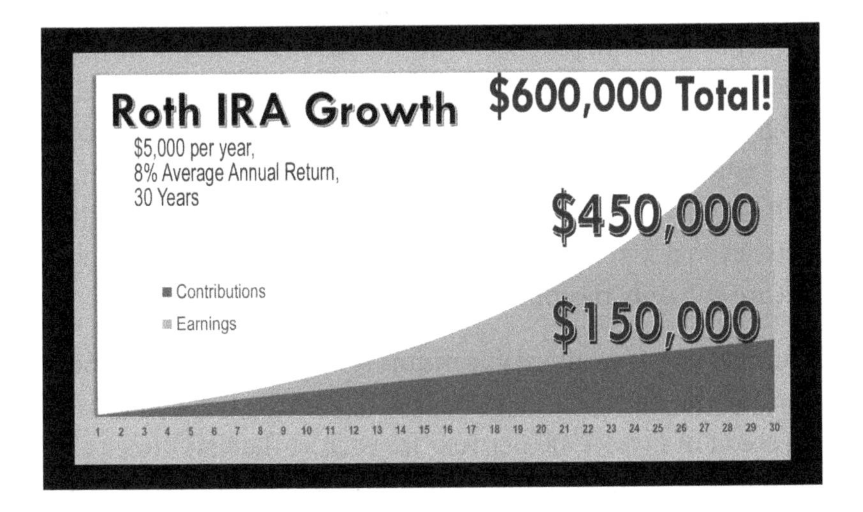

Unlike traditional IRAs, Roth IRAs are not subject to RMD during your lifetime. In other words, you can allow the funds in your Roth IRA to continue to grow if you do not need them for living expenses and pass them along to your heirs as part of your estate.

Eligibility Requirements for 2020:

- Married filing joint tax return: Reduced contributions if combined earnings are greater than $196,000
- $206,000 or more makes you ineligible to contribute to a Roth IRA
- Single Filers: the eligibility range for contributions is $124,000 to $139,000

SIMPLE IRA

A Savings Incentive Match Plan for Employees (SIMPLE) IRA is a good start-up plan for small dental practices that do not currently sponsor a retirement plan. This gives you the opportunity as the practice owner to save for retirement while incentivizing employees to do the same through a matching program. For example, you may agree to match up to 3 percent of an employee's pre-tax contribution for each eligible employee. If the employee contributes 2 percent of salary, the practice matches that 2 percent. If an employee contributes 10 percent, you are still only responsible for matching 3% as agreed.

A Simple IRA is an affordable means of establishing a retirement plan for you and your employees and you may be eligible for a tax credit of up to $500 per year for each of the first three years for the cost of starting the plan although administrative costs are very low.

Any money that you contribute for employees as part of the match is deductible as a business expense, which is a further benefit and incentive for practice owners.

Employees have control of their retirement savings, the election of funds and may roll over their funds to a traditional IRA or another employer's retirement plan at any time.

The downside to a Simple IRA is that even if the practice is not doing as well as expected, you are still required to make contributions to your employee's accounts according to a friend of mine who owns a practice in New Jersey. Although you can change the contribution amount, you must advise participants in writing of the change and it must not be below 1%.

SIMPLE IRA accounts must be opened by October 1 to make contributions for that tax year.

SEP IRA

A Simplified Employee Pension (SEP) IRA is a good choice for solo practitioners or those with just a few employees. Contributions are paid directly into an IRA created for each employee, and the same investment, distribution and rollover rules as a traditional IRA apply. Contributions to a SEP are tax-deductible, and the practice pays no taxes on the earnings on the investments. The employee is also free to supplement the SEP-IRA with another retirement plan.

A SEP IRA is very simple to set-up and maintains with minimal administrative costs and no annual filing requirements.

Unlike a Simple IRA, you are not locked into making annual contributions. In fact, you decide each year whether, and how much, to contribute to your employees' SEP-IRAs. The employer is responsible for 100% of the contributions to a SEP IRA since employees themselves cannot contribute. For an independent contractor, this is a great tool for saving for the future.

For an employer with multiple employees participating, the only restriction is that the percentage of the contribution must be equal for all participants.

The advantage for independent contractors is that a SEP IRA has much higher contribution limits than either a traditional or Roth IRA. You can contribute up to 25% of your compensation or a maximum of $57,000 for 2020. Withdrawals from a SEP IRA are taxed as ordinary income in retirement, and RMD rules apply.

Retirement Planning as an Independent Contractor

As an independent contractor, you are considered to be running your own business. You can choose (and pay for) your benefits and plan for retirement through a Solo 401K. You do not have to be worried about plan fees or often poor investment options by others.

You can make an "employee" contribution as well as an "employer" contribution up to 20% of your net annual income or $57,000 per year for the 2020 tax year. Be sure to check with the IRS regulations to confirm the contribution limits for this year.

To be eligible to contribute to this plan, you do not need to form an LLC or corporation but by the nature of being an independent contractor and receiving a 1099, you are automatically a sole proprietor and therefore, eligible to start a Solo 401K plan. The goal is to start young and maximize your contributions every year, putting into your retirement account the maximum allowable by the IRS.

Back Door Roth IRA

A backdoor Roth IRA is a way for people with high incomes to sidestep a traditional IRA limit and contribute extra money into their retirement, hence why it's labeled "backdoor". In fact, it is a very complicated method for high-income taxpayers to fund a Roth even if their income is higher than the maximum allowed per IRS regulations. It involves converting a traditional IRA into a Roth and should only be considered with the guidance of a broker or financial advisor.

The problem is that high-income earners are not allowed to fund a Roth IRA. However, traditional IRAs don't have these income limits. The basis for the Roth started in 2010 when income limits restricting the conversion of a traditional IRA to a Roth IRA were eliminated, giving way to this new "backdoor" option.

How to contribute to a back-door Roth IRA:

- Contribute money to an existing traditional IRA and then roll over the funds to a Roth IRA account.
- Convert your entire traditional IRA account to a Roth IRA account.
- Make an after-tax contribution to a Solo 401(k) plan and then roll it over to a Roth IRA

NOTE:

Taxes will be due on any money in your traditional IRA that hasn't already been taxed.

Taxes must be paid on any earnings between the time you contributed to the traditional IRA and when it was converted to a Roth IRA.

If you are under 59 ½, you have to wait five years to have penalty-free access to your funds unlike usual Roth IRA contributions, which you can withdraw at any time without taxes or penalties.

Unlike a Roth IRA, there are no income limits to be eligible to open an account.

Unlike a Roth IRA, there are no contribution limits.

The main advantage of a back-door IRA is that taxes are paid upfront on your contributions, and therefore, the money will be tax-free when you withdraw it sometime in the future. You may want to consider a back-door IRA if you think tax rates will rise in the future, or that your taxable income will be higher after you retire than it is now.

HSA account

Another option for retirement savings is to use a Health Savings Account (HSA). It gives you an upfront tax break like a 401(k), and it also provides for tax-free withdrawals if the money is used for health care. This makes it the most tax-advantaged retirement account available. If you do not use it for health care, you can withdraw the money penalty-free after age 65. However, you will still need to pay taxes on the withdrawn funds like a 401(k).

Life Insurance as a Savings Policy

As I discussed in Chapter 4, life insurance can be an excellent way to increase your savings for retirement.

Term life insurance is the best choice for most individuals and those just starting out. It is the least expensive type of life insurance and leaves money free for other savings options or investments. There is no cash value to a term life insurance policy and no investment components. In other words, low premiums for a significant death benefit for your beneficiary.

Permanent life insurance is more expensive than term but also allows policyholders to accumulate cash value. As long as you continue to pay the premiums, the policy continues to grow tax-deferred until you withdraw the funds. You may also borrow against the cash value of the policy in certain instances such as to buy a house, pay for college expenses, and even to pay for certain medical expenses.

There is an option that some people refer to called "buy term and invest the difference." In other words, buy regular term life insurance rather than a permanent policy with a more expensive premium. Then apply the difference in cost into an investment fund of some kind (i.e. index fund). You have the benefit of the immediate term life insurance benefits with the lower premium and the long-term benefit of the permanent policy by investing on your own.

An index fund for example may grow faster than a cash value policy. However, a permanent policy provides a predictable and stable return, unlike the stock market which can be unpredictable and unstable.

Stocks vs. Mutual Funds vs. Bonds

Investment options in stocks, mutual funds, and bonds are another excellent way of building a nest egg for the future. Your choices are dependent upon how much risk you are willing to take.

When you buy a **stock**, you are owning a share of the corporation. Stocks that offer dividends will pay you taxable income either quarterly or annually. When you sell your stock, you will also earn as long as the selling price is higher than what you paid for it less any fees. Stocks trade continuously, and the prices change throughout the day. If the market crashes, you can get out anytime during the trading session.

When it comes to **mutual funds**, you own a share of the mutual fund. The price of each mutual fund share is called its net asset value or the total value of all the securities it owns divided by the number of the mutual fund's shares. Mutual fund shares are traded continuously, but their prices adjust at the end of each business day. Unfortunately, this situation is certainly not optimal during times when the market is falling (like during a pandemic!) Many investors prefer mutual funds over stock since they are less risky.

Stocks are riskier than mutual funds. Many financial advisors recommend diversifying your portfolio between stocks and mutual funds to spread out and reduce the amount the risk.

Investing can be a confusing and challenging subject especially if your brain is not necessarily wired around finances. To fully comprehend the ins and outs of investing would require you to research individual companies, learn to read financial reports, and understand the many fees and costs associated with trading stocks. While a broker will charge you a fee when you buy or sell, and mutual funds will charge annual management fees, it is better to use the services of a broker and/or financial advisor so that you know you that what you are doing is in your best interest with your money.

Bonds are a very different story altogether. In contrast to stocks and mutual funds, bonds represent units of corporate debt issued by companies and securitized as tradable assets. They are considered to be a fixed income instrument since they traditionally pay a fixed interest rate (coupon) to debt holders.

Bond prices are inversely correlated with interest rates: when rates go up, bond prices fall and vice-versa. Bonds have maturity dates at which point the principal amount must be paid back in full or risk default.

A government, corporation, or other entity that needs to raise cash will borrow money in the public market and subsequently pay interest on that loan to investors. Upon maturity, the investor is returned the full amount of their original principal. Bonds do not have the same long-term income earnings as stocks, but they are preferred by investors for whom income is a priority. Also, bonds are less risky than stocks.

Many people invest in both stocks and bonds to diversify but this depends upon your tolerance for risk and the amount of time that you can leave your money in investments. To learn more about stocks, mutual funds, and bonds, be sure to check with a financial advisor or broker. Additional information can be found at www.thebalance.com.

Should I Keep Any Cash Savings?

As we discussed earlier, there are many philosophies for managing and budgeting your finances. When you consider what to do with your money, be sure to keep a portion of your earnings in CASH as an emergency fund and savings. You never know what life will bring you (i.e. COVID-19).

Most financial advisors advise keeping enough cash in your savings to cover at least 6 months' worth of expenses or 15 – 20% of your income. The point of an emergency fund is that the money is easily accessible whenever you need it. Whether that means leaving the money in a savings account or an investment account that may earn a higher rate of interest, be sure that you can retrieve the money quickly in case of an emergency.

To retire comfortably and live a lifestyle that you want after you stop working, you will need to have money in the bank and investments. Some financial professionals recommend $6M - $8M but this certainly depends upon your lifestyle, where in the country you live, and how you would like to live once you retire.

Ultimately, the goal is to invest your money into income-producing, dividend-paying investments that will help you to afford the lifestyle you worked so hard all your working career to achieve.

Ideally, you should have a diversified portfolio where you place your savings including Roth and other types of investment vehicles, stocks, bonds, and mutual funds. At the time of retirement, you do not liquidate all of it and stash it away. Those investments will continue to earn and pay you an income throughout the remainder of your life.

The market fluctuates regularly with changes in the financial and economic climate of the world. With the recent events associated with the COVID-19 pandemic, the markets tanked significantly However, this may be a good time to invest in the market as prices are low and the assumption and hope are that the market will rebound with time and take off.

Again, the amount of money that you invest in the financial vehicles will depend upon how much liquidity you desire to keep in reserves and your tolerance of risk. If you are conservative, you may want to keep more money in a savings account for a rainy day and less in investments. On the other hand, if you are young and are willing to take more risk, you may consider putting more money into your investments and riding the waves that traditionally occur with the market over a long period.

Personal Note:

For my savings/retirement plan, I have been working with Northwest Mutual. A colleague introduced me to his friend working for them and that's how I got started. They have been a solid group, with fiduciary responsibilities and good returns. There are plenty of options out there so look around and know you can always change groups at any time if you aren't content.

I currently contribute a yearly amount towards my SEP-IRA which Northwest Mutual manages and invests. I try to contribute the maximum amount I possibly can, as it adds to the retirement portfolio and what NWM has to play with. Also, because the higher contributions also help reduce the taxes I have to pay for that year. It can be a balancing act sometimes; if you are saving towards a big purchase (such as a house, practice, etc) that requires cash payment, then contributing too much can empty your bank account and leave you too little free cash for your purchase. However, keeping excessive cash income in your account each year also means you will pay extra taxes on that income (based on your bracket). You may be better off investing the money and earning a return, paying less in taxes for the year rather than staring at it through your online banking statement.

Regarding the investments themselves, I have focused on index funds, as they have shown the best and most consistent rate of return over time, as referenced again in the FRONTLINE documentary I recommended earlier and plenty of other financial studies.

Also, to reiterate, I have the whole life permanent life insurance policy as a further long-term investment as well. I have tried to maximize my disability as much as possible to protect against a worst-case scenario. The more diversity you can have in your savings and retirement options and your worst-case scenario plan, the better!

PART THREE

Owning your own Practice

6

Universal Essentials to Purchasing

"Measure twice, cut once"
~ anonymous

"ABC.... Always. Be. Closing."
~ Alec Baldwin, Glengarry GlenRoss

If you could practice a technique called "dreamlining," where you imagine your ideal dental career scenario for the next 6 months, one year, 5 years, and 10 years, what would it be? Everyone is completely different, but the realistic options that exist today are the following: Associate, own/start practice from scratch, purchase an existing solo practice, join/buy into a DSO (corporate/chain), teach.

Although there are several options available to you, the majority of us fall into the following game plan:

Graduate school. Work as an associate to get experience 1-5yrs, buy/open an office, maybe buy more practices, bring an associate on board and cut back, sell, retire.

How did I do? Regardless of the situation, for most of us, there is one goal in common: **Owning a practice**. It's the ultimate dream and top of the pyramid for our field. Finally, a place where I get to do things *my way*, on *my terms*, with full control.

How does your dream practice look? 2 chairs? 5 chairs? Solo? Multi-specialty? Not all practices are created equal, and I certainly don't have a magic formula for each of your individual scenarios. What I can provide in this section are the statistics you will need to know before you purchase your first practice and the ones you will need to consider once you are an owner.

Now, I'm not a practice owner myself and have no desire to (more on that later), so my dreamline is likely totally different than the majority.

So how do I qualify to tell you what to consider and what pitfalls and factors to pay close attention to? I couldn't agree more, and that's why I've asked several friends who have personally gone through every scenario to share their wisdom first-hand.

Some were hesitant at first; why share the inside info they were never taught and had to learn the hard way? Dental ownership is tough, and they have the scars to show it. That's why having them share their knowledge is a priceless resource.

Dental Practice Ownership

Of the many dentists and practice owners with whom I spoke to gather information for this book, there was one resounding theme from all of them. Do NOT start a dental practice from scratch! You will be faced with heartaches, challenges, hardships, and headaches. You will incur a lot of additional overhead (which we will address in the next chapter) with no guarantees of patients walking in the door. You will spend the first several years at a minimum just establishing your reputation in the community.

All of the experienced dentists who I spoke with recommended thorough research into purchasing an existing dental practice as the best alternative if you want to be an owner. While it is important to note that none of them recommended starting a business from nothing, the most important comment that I heard was research – do your due diligence! You want to have as much information as possible at your fingertips so that you can make an informed decision. Since this decision will determine your financial and professional success, you certainly want to put in as much time and energy as is possible to ensure that you do not regret your decision 2, 3, or 10 years down the road.

Step 1: Organize a team of specialized dental advisers

The first step is to gather the following team of specialized advisers to assist you with very specific steps in the process:

Dental Attorney - Non-compete provisions, Re-treatment clauses, securely transferring patient records, as well as the purchase and collection of accounts receivable (AR).

Dental CPA – To determine the financial health of the practice that you are purchasing and evaluate expenses, insurance, patient payment history, rent, and liabilities, etc.

Transition Consultant (the buying dentist's adviser) - Employee management, Patient retention, Regulatory compliance, Dental Software, Effective communications.

Professional Practice Lender - Dental-specific lenders are more flexible and may grant you a loan with less collateral even if you have high student loans.

Consultant – Most dentists are not business people. We went to dental school, not business school, hence why you are reading this book. If you are uncomfortable (as you should be) with any of these decisions, documents, or terms, there are certainly business consultants that can guide you and direct you to make the best, most appropriate business decision for YOU. Of course, this comes with a cost but you must weigh out the costs/benefits associated with taking the leap of faith and buying a practice or sitting back and wondering "what if". Hiring a consultant is not a sign of weakness as a business owner but rather a sign that you are interested in making the best decision to earn the most profit.

Step 2: Make an offer to the seller and submit a letter of intent (LOI)

After you and your advisers are comfortable with the practice's prospectus and potential, the next step is to submit a signed letter of intent to the selling dentist. A letter of intent, which is typically non-binding, is a way of communicating to the seller that you are serious about buying their practice. The more you and the seller can agree upon in the letter of intent, the smoother the sales transaction will be. At a minimum, the following terms should be addressed in the LOI:

- What assets are to be included in the sale?
- What assets will be excluded from the sale?

- The practice purchase price
- The expected closing date

An LOI can be as short as one page or consist of multiple pages, but it is generally shorter than a definitive purchase agreement. It is generally best that a letter of intent includes certain non-binding terms allowing for further negotiation, and others that are binding including confidentiality and the removal of the practice from the market while negotiations are taking place.

The Letter of Intent should include:

- **Proposed purchase price.** How much do you want to offer for the practice? Include whether this price is for equity or assets as well as if it includes stock options.
- **Accounts receivable (AR).** Will the accounts receivable (the amount currently due to the practice from patients) be purchased and will any discounts be accepted. It is important to determine if payments for work completed will be assigned to the new owner or if they will be submitted as income to the previous owner after the closing date.
- **Assets.** The Letter of Intent should specifically identify all assets (whether they are used for revenue-generation or not) that are included and/or excluded with the sale of the business.
- **Debt and liability.** The existing practice owner is selling the business yet will still be responsible for any outstanding debt or contractual obligations. All liabilities and credits should be clearly defined in the LOI.

- **Noncompete agreements.** If there are any noncompete guidelines such as geographical restrictions (miles from the practice) and time restrictions (years in which the non-compete will be valid), they should be included in the original LOI.
- **Lease agreement.** Identify the current lease agreement for the office space and specifically indicate that the sale of the practice is contingent upon the successful assignment or execution of a new lease for the office space.
- **Re-treatments.** The letter of intent should include who is responsible for the retreatment of patients and how much the new owner will earn if he/she performs the services.
- **Access to financial records and due diligence.** The current owner must give access to the potential buyer to evaluate the practice and its financials. Be sure to look at current expenses and spending habits, rent, utilities, the cost of payroll, etc.
- **Confidentiality.** Both the buyer and seller must be bound to the terms of confidentiality.
- **Exclusivity.** As the buyer, you are putting a lot of effort into the terms of sale and negotiations. You want to make sure that the seller is not negotiating with another potential buyer during the process.
- **Employment.** In some cases, the seller is interested in selling the business but wants to remain on as an employee. This arrangement should be spelled out in the LOI if applicable.
- **Expense.** Be clear in the LOI that each party is responsible for any expenses incurred in legal fees, etc. during this business transaction.

- **Closing date.** Do your best to provide an estimated date that the final sales transaction will occur. Of course, this is dependent upon other factors as well so provide a rough date if possible.

- **Expiration date.** Set a date approximately ten days into the future at which time the LOI will expire if no further action is taken on the sale/purchase of the practice.

- **Transition period.** If you are planning on arranging for a transition period between the owner phasing out and you gradually phasing in, then that period should also be mentioned in the contract. Ideally, a set amount of time and dates should be included; the more specifics you have the better. If, however, you want a more "open" period, then that can work too. But there should still be a set period (6 months to 1 year) established where you as the new owner can plan on being the only boss. Having the previous owner there during a transition can be a big help, especially with patients who are more reluctant with the new ownership; having the previous owner stick around indefinitely and come and go as he/she pleases is NOT a good idea and can potentially result in friction and affect your authority as the new owner.

Step 3: Apply for a practice purchase loan from the bank

After you have submitted your letter of intent, the next step is to get pre-qualified for a practice purchase loan. Your dental attorney or CPA should be able to put you in touch with several local banks or professional practice lenders.

How to Fund Your Practice

Now, we know you're wondering where you're going to come up with the money it takes to start a dental practice.

In most cases, you will need to apply for a loan.

This means you start by writing an excellent business plan to show to the potential investors and banks where you apply for a loan.

- Break down your timeline, the costs, your expected profits, how many people you will hire, and your industry experience.
- Ensure that your credit report is as strong as possible. You can check your credit history through one if not all of the credit reporting agencies (Experian, TransUnion, and Equifax)
- Apply for a loan with many different lenders, and remember that the interest rate is often actually more important than the amount of money that you're offered. You want to be sure that you will be able to get out of the debt that you're putting yourself in. Another benefit of applying for multiple loans is that you might even be able to leverage one offer against another competing bank's offer.

Buying a dental practice is a very big decision and one that should not be rushed. Be patient and be sure to speak with a financial advisor and an accountant before making any final decisions. It is important to review the practice's financials beforehand and speak with the bookkeeper and/or accountant to get a full picture of the current state of the practice.

Some dentists fear that they will never qualify for a practice loan due to their substantial student debt. The truth of the matter is, if you're a dentist with at least one year of experience, a decent credit score, and demonstrated ability to ability to create production, chances are good you won't have a problem getting a loan.

Banks think of dentists as a low-risk loan. Dentistry is profitable and dentists nearly always pay back their loans. For this reason, if you look at buying a healthy dental practice and you have a decent credit history, you should not have a problem getting a good loan. Whether or not you get the loan will all come down to cash flow. Does the revenue that the practice collects after paying expenses cover not just your personal debts but leave you enough to live on?

Choosing which loan proposal you are going to accept will be the next challenge. Several banks have dental-specific lending arms. These groups understand the unique economics of dental practices and lend accordingly.

How much can you borrow?

Generally speaking, dental lenders will lend 100% of the purchase price of the practice plus and an additional amount for either working capital or money to purchase the accounts receivable. This is true at nearly every bank one of my dental colleagues approached with one crucial detail to take note of; the 85% rule.

Banks will rarely lend a total of 85% of the prior year's collections to buy a practice.

Put another way, if a practice collected exactly $1,000,000 last year, and you're buying the practice, the maximum amount that banks will lend you is $850,000 for the purchase price AND anything additional, like working capital, money to purchase the accounts receivable or to purchase new equipment.

The 85% number is definitely a rule of thumb, and generally the top limit.

Practices should (always a dangerous word) sell for much less than that, on average. If you're borrowing 85% of the previous year's collections, you're probably buying a premium, top-of-the-line practice as a friend of mine who has been practicing for many years told me.

For additional information on the types of bank loans that dentists are eligible for and what banks look for in the lending process, be sure to check out https://practicefinancialgroup.com/get-bank-loan-purchase-dental-practice/

It is a good idea to submit applications to several banks, as not all banks have the same interest rates or loan terms. Therefore, you must start the pre-qualification process early on so that you can secure funding in time to meet the closing date you have specified in your letter of intent.

Here is a shortlist of some of the most common documents that banks request in the underwriting process:

- A signed Dental Practice Purchase and Sale Agreement
- A signed lease agreement or assignment (with a term equal to the length of loan)
- Corporate documents, including articles of incorporation and tax ID number
- Life and disability insurance policies

When considering the loan term, keep in mind the duration of the loan. Consider the longest term available (for example, 10 to 15 years) allowing you to minimize the payments while you are growing the business. If your business does better than expected, you can always pay down the loan early. Pre-payment options vary from lender to lender and there is typically no pre-payment penalty.

Interest Rates can be fixed for the term or adjust with prime or other rate indexes. Although payments may be lower with an adjustable-rate, rates will eventually rise, so locking in a competitive fixed rate for the next seven to 15 years is your best solution.

Step 4: Insurance Policies

As was discussed in detail in Chapter 4, your dental practice must acquire various types of insurance to operate including:

- Malpractice insurance
- Life insurance
- Disability insurance
- General business liability insurance
- Personal property insurance

Many of these documents must be presented to the bank or lending institution as a requirement of your loan.

Step 5: Type of business

It is important that you establish the dental practice according to state guidelines. Be sure to review the various types of businesses and tax ramifications as discussed in Chapter 3.

Step 6: Have a dental attorney review dental practice purchase agreement

The Practice Purchase Agreement is the contract that will ultimately lay out the terms of the sale/purchase of the dental practice. This document must be created by and reviewed by a practicing Dental attorney to ensure that each party can comply with the specific details of the sale. Some of the items that are addressed in the purchase agreement include:

- The seller and buyer's respective representations and warranties
- The assets that are included (or excluded) in the sale
- Who will control the patient records?
- The scope of the restrictive covenant (time and geographic distance)
- The collecting of the seller's accounts receivable and patient credits
- Procedure for handling any *re-do's* or retreatments
- Allocation of the purchase price for tax purposes
- Ongoing contractual obligations or liabilities
- Status of employees
- The transition letter notifying patients that the practice has been sold

Step 7: Office Space

If you will be continuing the practice in the same location, you must review and negotiate in the purchase agreement the specific details and terms of the lease or real estate owned by the practice. You may even want to have an attorney look at the lease to ensure that you understand the terms including the termination date, the frequency and rate of increases, the ability to renew, and the areas of responsibility of the landlord. Most importantly, you want to ensure that the lease is transferable. In other words, when you decide to sell the practice at some time later in life, you want to ensure that the new owner can continue to operate the business in the same location. This is done through a transfer clause. If possible, you should build a good rapport with the landlord to ensure that everyone "lives in harmony".

The seller should notify the landlord of the intent to sell the practice as early as possible and verify that the landlord will consent to the transition of the lease to the new owner.

If the lease is to be renegotiated, keep in mind that the term of the lease must be equal to the length of the purchase loan with the bank.

Step 8: Sign documents/ownership transition

All of the documents and the agreement must be signed by all parties and will then be submitted to the bank to finalize the underwriting. The funds will be transferred to the seller upon completion.

Once all of the requirements contained in the agreement are met and the seller has received funds from the lending institution, you can take possession of the practice and make any notifications to staff and patients.

Step 9: Send out a transition letter to patients

Once the sale is final, you as the new owner must notify patients of the change in ownership as well as the transition plan. Be sure to assure them that they should not expect any change in the quality of service that they receive. They will be curious about your experience and credentials as well as your plans for the practice.

Be sure to express the confidence that the previous owner has in you as well as thank them for their continued patronage.

Step 10: Tie Up Loose Ends

As with any business transition, there will always be a few loose ends that will need to be tied up:

- **Firing and Hiring:** It is customary for the selling dentist to terminate the contract with their existing employees and for you as the new owner to rehire them if so desired.
- **Pro-rata Adjustments:** If the practice purchase closes sometime after the 1st of the month, there will likely be some unpaid utilities or other service contracts. Liability for paying these mid-cycle bills is often split pro-rata but must be defined in the purchase agreement.
- **Licenses and Registrations:** Transfer or update all local, state, and federal licenses and registrations from the seller's name into your name.

Average Cost of Purchasing a Practice

Over the last few years, the average selling price for an existing dental practice has been between $350,000 – $550,000. A practice in Boston, Los Angeles, San Francisco, or New York City may be double to even triple these numbers. That being said, I am hesitant to give you these general numbers since there are so many factors involved with the purchase price of a practice.

Overall, the two main factors that determine that cost are your *region and your square footage.*

Be sure that where you purchase the practice is a match with your personal and professional goals. Your future success and the ease at which you'll reach it are closely related to your choice of region.

- Consider purchasing a practice in an affordable area based on what you can afford NOW, not what you hope to be able to afford in the future.

In other words, make sure that your vision and financial goals align with the size of the practice, location, square footage, etc.

The following are some estimates and will vary whether you are purchasing an existing practice or starting your own.

Square Footage Needed: 2000

Construction: $240,000 (leasehold improvements – costs vary 30-40% based on your area of the country but this example uses $120 per square foot – should calculate $25,000 to $100,000 in a free construction allowance provided by the landlord)

- Equipment, supplies, IT, software and furniture: $190,000
- Working Capital (marketing, payroll, consultant, legal, accounting, website, rent, etc.) – $70,000
- Total start-up costs are $500,000

Size	3-chair 1,800 sq. ft	6-chair 2,925 sq. ft	9-chair 3,490 sq. ft
Patients Treated/Year	1,472-1,619	2,944-3,238	3,754-4,858
Visits/Year (DDS+DH)	3,680-4,048	7,360-8,096	9,384-12,144
Start-up Costs			
Remodeling ($148/sq. ft)			
Construction ($215/sq. ft)	$387,000	$628,875	$750,370
Large Equipment	$156,320	$312,640	$468,960
Supplies, Instruments, and Small Equipment	$47,795	$70,590	$93,385
Annual Operating Costs			
Staff (w/o benefits) Dir. $147,361/Staff $125,882	1 $147,361	2 $273,243	3 $399,125
Dental assistant Average salary $35,621	2 $71,242	4 $142,484	6 $213,726
Dental hygienist Average salary $70,425	0.5 $35,212	1 $70,425	1.5 $105,637
Clerical/receptionist Average salary $33,588	1 $33,588	1 $33,588	1 $33,588
Practice manager Average salary $67,225	0	1 $67,255	1 $67,255
Utilities average $9,467 to $12,924	$9,467	$10,619	$11,723
Rent or mortgage payment average $31,212	$29,238	$30,408	$33,000
Dental supplies $8/ visit for fixed clinic	$32,384	$64,768	$97,152
Other (charts, office supplies) $2,611 to $5,762	$2,611	$3,986	$4,856
Total start-up costs	$591,115	$1,012,105	$1,312,715
Total annual operating costs	$361,103	$696,776	$966,062
Total first-year costs	$952,218	$1,708,881	$2,278,777

Specialty	Average FMV/Collections	Average Goodwill/Purchase Price	Average Tangible Assets/Purchase Price	Number of Transactions
General Dentistry	69.87%	76.10%	23.90%	428
Orthodontics	79.81%	68.59%	31.41%	202
Oral Surgery	68.57%	74.41%	25.59%	53
Pediatric Dentistry	71.22%	81.05%	18.95%	69
Periodontics	65.62%	77.63%	22.37%	39
Endodontics	67.61%	82.18%	17.82%	15
Prosthodontics	67.13%	67.06%	32.94%	9

The above dental clinic comparison chart figures are based on 2016 statistics of dental practices.

To better understand how to evaluate the cost of purchasing a dental practice, I asked another friend for advice on this subject. He recommended looking at the average of the last three years' gross income into the business. Of course, this does not take into consideration patients who may leave or new ones who you may attract but it is a very fair way of calculating what the business is worth to someone coming in to make an offer.

The role of staff in purchasing a practice

How many staff members are there in the existing practice? Are they employees or independent contractors (e.g. associates and possibly hygienists)? Do they have written contracts in place? Is there any ongoing litigation, proceedings, claims – threatened or real – involving the employees? How long have they been there? What are their roles? Will they be staying on after the purchase and sale are completed?

By gathering some initial information, you'll be in a much better position to not only plan for employment-related matters AFTER the deal finishes but also mitigate your employment-related risks leading up to the deal finishing!

In theory, by keeping existing team members on board for at least a few months, you can enjoy a smooth, pleasant transition into your new role as a practice owner. Patients will appreciate seeing familiar faces and you can gain valuable insight regarding the practice's strengths and opportunities for improvement. Ideally, you should also negotiate with the previous owner to stay on board for six months to a year to assist with the transition as an associate, allowing both patients and employees to get to know you and your style as the new owner and dentist.

Tips to a smooth employee transition

1. Arrange to spend a few days onsite to understand how the existing staff interacts with one another and patients. Shadow the current staff to gain insight into their work ethics and behaviors.

2. It is natural for employees to be worried about their jobs and fearful of impending changes that may lie ahead. Schedule a meeting that includes the outgoing practice owner as well as the existing team members to discuss your intentions, your goals, and vision for the practice. This may help to alleviate some of the fears and stress that employees have about the transition.

3. Meet with team members and ask them about their jobs to determine if they will be a good fit for you and your practice.

4. Clearly define your goals and expectations for the business as well as from each of the team members.

5. Ideally, the team of employees that you put together will flourish and work well together moving forward. However, it is always a good idea to evaluate how well each employee is performing after 90 days of working for you.

6. Introduce a company handbook that documents your policies and expectations.
7. Existing employees frequently want to know how their employment, pay, and benefits package will be impacted by the sale of the business.

Cautionary tale:

I have had several colleagues who have bought/taken over an existing practice from an owner who was there many years and retained staff. The staff was very upset about the change in ownership, despite no fault of the new owner. The result in each case was in-office staff that no longer worked with the same level of dedication and motivation as before; in fact, many of the retained staff began working ***directly against*** the new owner.

This might sound odd, but they were so attached to a certain doctor in a certain way of doing things that they simply were not willing to make the necessary changes based on the new owner's wishes. The result was a prolonged transition and stressful office environment which eventually led to multiple firings with dramatic Post-fire bouts of anger and sabotage, including even phantom one-star posts on sites such as Yelp.

Therefore, it would be worth considering retaining the previous owner for a minimum of six months to one year in some cases to encourage and work directly with the staff to help them during the transition. Sometimes it may also work well to aid you with consults and treatment planning, depending on your experience and how much you are looking to learn from the prior owner. Especially in cases where patients have been used to seeing one dentist for several decades, it's probably to your benefit to have that same dentist introduce you to patients. This will help to reassure them that the practice is in great hands rather than having them show up to an abrupt changing of the guard and a new face. It also, therefore, behooves you as the new owner to have as positive of a relationship with the previous owner as possible. Having an ugly negotiation period may likely result in an ugly transition period.

Thus, think long and hard about how you want your transition period to look, and also, take into consideration the possibility of needing to "start fresh" with staff and managers of YOUR choosing who come in with a positive attitude and are not tied up to past loyalties. This may take time, but if there are some obvious signs of resentment from prior staff right away, then each day you delay could cause you a significant headache in the future.

Location, Location, Location

"Choosing location is integral to the film: in essence, another character"
~ Ridley Scott - Oscar award-winning Film Director and producer

"Silicon Valley is a mindset, not a location."
~ Reid Hoffman - Entrepreneur and venture capitalist, Co-founder LinkedIn

This is the most debatable section of the book. Where you choose to work will have huge ramifications on every other aspect of your personal life. But from a purely business standpoint (since this is what this book is about), there is no debate: choosing where to open, purchase, or join a practice is a major X-factor in the game. Choose well, and your chances for success are high; choose poorly, and all the best dentistry and marketing in the world may not be enough to save you.

Like all cases, there is a ton to consider and there is no one-size-fits-all formula, but I want to help provide a few important tips to keep in mind to determine if your location is good or not.

- **Demographics** - Who is your ideal patient? Research the population in the region surrounding your potential new location to identify the average household income, the consistency of the population, and the average age of the population.
    - Household income will play a role in the forms of payment that you accept as well as the type of procedures that may be done. For example, is your practice in a low-income area in which patients may not have insurance or may not be able to pay? On the other hand, do they have more discretionary income and can afford cosmetic dental procedures?
    - Is the population in the area growing or are people moving away? Is the city growing and are there opportunities to attract new patients?
    - What is the average age of the population? Are there a lot of families with children and therefore a pediatric dental specialty will be beneficial? Or is the population older requiring more prosthetic work?
- **Consider Non-Competes** - Where did you work before your venture into ownership? Do you have a restrictive covenant in your previous employment agreement? You may be restricted from owning a dental practice within a predetermined number of miles from your previous place of employment. If you are a dental student or associate, consider associateship placement ten plus miles away from your ideal location so that you can prevent running into an issue with your restrictive covenant when it's time to buy a dental practice.

- **Building Type** - When you zero in on a dental practice for sale, consider the type of building that it is currently in. Is it in a stand-alone building, a shopping center, or in a medical community? While there are pros and cons to each of these choices, your decision may be based on personal preference as well as marketing and visibility options. For example, having an independent building for your practice can make the business a bit more distinctive, ensure you have a unique address, and allow you to have more control over your signage options. But being located in a shopping center offers advertising opportunities and may allow your practice to stand out amongst retail locations and restaurants. Being situated in a medical building can offer a sense of community and even increase your referral potential; it can also help you reach certain patients and gain some loyalty recognition, yet it may also result in increased competition as well.
- **Visibility** - Keep in mind that the type of building you choose may also influence how visible your practice is from the main road, what kind of marketing you may need, and how convenient parking will be for patients. For general practitioners who do not typically depend on a referral source for patients, you want to consider how well the location allows potential patients to see and access your practice.
- **Signage** – What type of signage is allowed based on your lease and/or rental agreement?
- **Zoning** - Confirm with the local building department that the existing location is commercially zoned and can be used for a dental practice. Since zoning regulations

change often, be sure to check on its status and file a zoning variance if necessary.

- **Parking** - Where are your patients going to park? What about your employees? Parking alone can be a significant draw/retractor for many practices.

- **Good family town** – The current demographics and projections will be very important in selecting a location. If your business is in a vibrant, growing community, there may be several other dental practices within a few miles of yours. That being the case, you will have to develop a way to differentiate your services from another.

- **Demographics** - The goal of using **demographic data** is to identify areas with individuals and families who fit the profile of your ideal patients including:

    - Average household size
    - Ethnicity
    - Median age
    - Median household income
    - Native language
    - Owner-or renter-occupied households
    - Households with private insurance

- **Density** - The goal of using **density data** is to understand the intensity of land use in an area (e.g., people per square mile or housing units per acre). To evaluate density data and how it will impact your practice, be sure to look at the following:

    - Population density (number of persons per square mile)
    - Total population
    - Population growth rate
    - Forecasted population growth rate
    - Number and type of housing units
    - Number and type of jobs

- **Competition** - According to the American Dental Association, a good **competition ratio** is one dentist to every 1,500 patients within a three to five-mile radius. But it also cautions you to be sure to look beneath the raw numbers. You should also consider if the existing practices are truly your competition and meeting patients' needs. **Are you planning on treating a different population base?** Areas with rapid growth or re-gentrification may have existing practices that may not be adapting to or serving the influx of new patients. **Will you be offering services not readily available?** Well-established practices may not offer new cosmetic dental procedures or advances in dental care. There could be an opportunity to serve a community that, on paper, appears to be oversaturated.
- **Real Estate Data** Once you have evaluated the demographic, density, and competition data, utilize local real estate data to narrow office options within those areas looking specifically at 3 qualities:
    - Is the practice located in a dominant position that can't be overshadowed by a competitor?
    - Is it located between homes and daily-needs stores?

- Does it have the potential for visibility and large, bright signage with exposure to traffic?

The majority of dental practices are located in shopping centers or near grocery stores for convenience as practices located near complementary businesses may reduce the need for marketing and serve to attract patients.

One dentist that I spoke to evaluated the demographics and density of the population in the area that he was considering purchasing a dental practice. He told me that generally, a number that would determine a reasonable patient base would be 3,000 to 4,000 people per mile per dentist. While there are other factors involved in determining if a location is viable and will prove to be profitable, this is a good indicator if you will be able to support the population and if you will have enough clients to support your business.

He also gave me great advice that I feel is critical and should be passed along to anyone considering purchasing or opening a dental practice. Do NOT rush!! Remember that you are making a long-term investment and commitment with your decision so you want to be sure that you select the right location to meet your financial goals and obligations. Typically, most lease agreements are for a term of 10 years so you want to be sure that you select the appropriate location that will support you and your business for at least 10 years.

Personal Note:

So, this isn't exactly a personal note, but more opinion on the rise of Dental Service Organizations (DSO's) and the direction our field seems to increasingly be headed towards. It seems like there has been a gradual shift over the past decade toward the DSO. They have slowly but surely started to gobble up massive swaths of territory and practices across the country. Several decades ago, the thought of a multi-specialty practice wasn't very common whereas today, in part thanks to the 2008 financial collapse, it's far more common. The same has started to happen with the DSO's to the point where some within our field argue that the solo dental practice will also slowly start to fade out as more and more corporations, backed by venture capital money, are taking hold of all industries including dentistry.

I have also seen a change in the mentality of dentists as well with the younger generation of clinicians. We tend to be more entrepreneurial and eager to look at expanding our practices with the ultimate goal of selling to a bigger group and calling it a career; prior generations were focused on their private practice and having a stable base to last their careers and provide for their families. While both approaches can have success, I think it's worth mentioning for anyone starting out to take this rise in the DSO seriously and to consider possible ramifications and long-term goals you may have for yourself with this in mind.

If you are looking to buy many practices to sell them at an older age, this may be a great opportunity for you (yet far, far easier said than done). If you are focused on growing one private practice for the long haul, do what you can to research and keep your eyes on the rearview mirror to see if the DSO train is passing through your area. Unfortunately, given their massive financial abilities, it could become increasingly difficult to compete against them if they decide to make an all-out push, especially in your area.

Remember the movie "You've Got Mail?" where Tom Hanks and his corporate book chain machine came into town and destroyed the competition of local mom and pop shops like the one Meg Ryan had? The process is not too far off from that...even the sound of it is similar: Instead of the catchphrase "F-O-X" from the film, simply exchange it for "D-S-O". However, unlike the film, for many of us, this may not have the same happy ending. Food for thought and something else to think about and consider depending on where you live and practice.

7

How high is the ceiling? Watching your overhead and essentials once you are an Owner

"Now the guy's got Paulie as a partner. Any problems, he goes to Paulie. Trouble with the bill? He can go to Paulie. Trouble with the cops, deliveries, Tommy, he can call Paulie. But now the guy's gotta come up with Paulie's money every week no matter what. Business bad? Pay me. Oh, you had a fire? Pay me. Place got hit by lightning, huh? Pay me."
~ Ray Liotta Goodfellas

Now that you are an office owner, it's all about running your business and building your empire. Again, I don't own one myself, but as an independent contractor, I have worked in over 15 different practices, so I've had more exposure to different types of practices than most of my colleagues.

From corporate to private, multi-specialty to specialty only, high-end, and more "cost-friendly", I have seen it all so I have a unique perspective of my own as to what factors make for a successful practice. The one universal factor that makes or breaks each of them, regardless of what kind it is, is managing the overhead.

Overhead costs are the invisible guillotine hanging over the head of every practice owner; month in and month out, whether the business is booming or tanking, your overhead fees will be there to greet you, and there is no hiding from them. From your office rent, to payroll, to air conditioning, even toilet paper, the list of expenses is very long, and can be very costly.

Thus, you need to be confident that your practice can produce enough to cover the bills, not to mention have extra to put money in your own pocket. Otherwise, the bank and everyone else will be coming for you, and you don't want to be in anyone's debt. Learn to manage your overhead like a skilled matador maneuvers a bull...or prepare to be gored.

Overhead

If you are purchasing a pre-existing business, you may already have all of the equipment that you need. As mentioned by other clinicians in previous chapters, it may be in your best interest NOT to start from scratch. Your overhead costs will be significantly higher because you will have to purchase EVERYTHING, which will significantly increase your expenses as well as possibly set you up for more debt.

For clarification's sake, let's look at the difference between dental equipment and dental supplies both of which are key components in your dental practice.

Dental equipment consists of bigger, investment pieces such as dental chairs and panoramic x-ray units while dental supplies are single-use items such as fluoride, floss, and gloves.

Whether you need to purchase all of the equipment for your practice or even add a few pieces, save yourself a ton of money and purchase refurbished or used dental equipment that is in good condition. While the large dealers like Henry Schein and Patterson will try to sell you top of the line, brand new equipment, you can certainly purchase previously owned equipment that will suit your needs just fine. Do not fall into the trap that some retailers will try to hook you with: New practice needs new equipment! You may regret it later when you are still paying down the debt that you owe on this equipment several years into your practice.

I did find a website that provides a new owner with practical information about dental equipment companies, products, and prices. Check out www.dentimax.com for some great ideas as to the type of equipment you will need as well as some resources to get you started to finding previously owned equipment.

Benchmark numbers for a practice

The following are some basic benchmark numbers that an average-sized dental practice owner should expect to budget for regularly. Of course, these do not take into consideration the cost of purchasing the practice, equipment costs, or any other debt that is acquired with the business.

Expense Category	Estimated Percentage
Rent or Mortgage	4-8%
Insurance	2%
Outside services	2.5%
Utilities	1%
Communication	1%
Payroll including taxes	20-24%
Marketing	2-5%
Continuing education	2%
Office Supplies	1-2%
Dental Supplies	5-7%
Lab Expenses	8-10%
Total Expenses	**48.5 – 64.5%**

Total Overhead costs for the average dentist are approximately 73%. Unfortunately, this does not leave much room for the owner's salary.

Of course, staffing and payroll are going to be your greatest expenses and may in fact exceed the amount that you owe to the bank each month for the purchase of the business. Payroll is something that has to be carefully evaluated and should make up no more than 20% of the business' overall budget. This includes salaries, worker's compensation, payroll taxes, and medical insurance. Although this is a large number, it is important to remember that without employees, you may not be able to earn any income or enough to earn a profit. So, as difficult as it is to have the staffing line item in your budget, remember that it is a controllable expense based on the number of staff and their respective salaries.

Every dentist that I have spoken to emphatically told me that payroll is by far the largest expense in their budget. In fact, the larger the practice, the larger the payroll.

As you balance out your budget, keep in mind that happy staff will always work in your best interest but money is not always a driving force in an employee's overall job satisfaction. In other words, do not simply throw money at an employee to make them more productive. This will only disrupt the delicate balance of your payroll and overhead budget while not necessarily change the amount of production earned.

The Indisputable Costs

Whether you buy or lease your practice location, you're going to have some large expenses from the get-go. There will more than likely be a lag time before your practice starts generating revenue. Let's look at some of the primary costs that you need to factor into your budget.

- Rent. Whether you are negotiating new lease terms or are extending the previous owner's contract, you will probably have to provide several months' rent and a security deposit upfront.
- Renovations: The current space may require some renovations to meet your specific needs so be sure to account for those in your preliminary budget.
- Dental Equipment: As discussed earlier, there is no need to purchase brand new equipment to either start or even refresh the dental equipment in the office. Do your homework and find the best deals on refurbished or used equipment when you can.
- Dental Supplies: These recurring expenses are critical to the operation and function of the business and must be budgeted into your calculations as regular monthly expenses.

- Lab Expenses/fees. While supplies are pretty consistent within a practice, lab fees are a huge part of overhead. More than 98% of dental practices include dental lab fees as part of their services. In other words, it is an expense that has to be accounted for out of your profits and these figures can be pretty significant.
- Staffing: Staffing and all associated payroll costs can be a significant chunk of your overall budget. Be sure to carefully evaluate the salaries and benefits of each employee that you will be hiring from the previous owner as well as to establish a baseline for bonuses and performance-based increases. One dentist that I spoke to expressed her surprise when discovered how high salaries expenses can be. "I was shocked at how much payroll was". Between all the payroll taxes, bonuses, and paid vacations, the payroll budget was huge. And of course, the more employees you have, the bigger the payroll will be."
- Marketing: If you are purchasing an existing practice, you may find yourself in the minority not having to do much marketing. You may be fortunate enough to be able to carry on the business with existing customers while organically attracting new ones by word of mouth. However, if you are looking to scale then you will certainly have to invest in marketing and advertising of your services.
- Operational Costs: You obviously have to turn the lights on, regulate the temperature, and pay the insurance expenses. These can certainly add up over time as well, especially if you aren't careful about turning off lights/ turning off equipment, etc. at the end of your workday.

Even if you think you have covered everything in your budget, there are always those costs that can easily be overlooked when it comes to operating your practice. I want to pull back the veil and make sure that these are not forgotten.

- Self-Employment Taxes: As the owner of the business and self-employed practitioner, you are responsible for paying Social Security and Medicare taxes as lump sum estimated payments. These taxes can be significant so be sure to budget for it.
- Health Insurance/Personnel Benefits: Health insurance premiums can be significant especially as a small business owner. You want to not only provide the best benefits possible to attract and retain employees but also to be consistent within your financial capabilities. Shop around!
- Vacation Time: As a small business owner, you must plan ahead and budget for vacation time for yourself and consider the time your staff may ask for days off. Also, don't forget the major holidays.
- Retirement: It is important to begin saving early in your career as was discussed in Chapter 5. Consider putting money in your budget to account for retirement savings.
- Repairs and Maintenance: Unfortunately, issues will arise and there is never a good time for it. The equipment in your office will require regular maintenance to keep it in tip-top shape and you should reserve funds to replace some of it as it ages and new technology comes out. You also want to be sure that you have funds in the budget to account for any unexpected problems that may occur because again, life happens!
- Routine/Daily Maintenance: You will need to have contracts with outside vendors to manage and collect your metal and your sharps, the HVAC, and the suction

lines. Although they are not daily activities, they are required maintenance activities that come with the territory. However, be sure to review your contracts with vendors to ensure that you are getting the best price to keep your expenses to a minimum.

- Miscellaneous: Things such as postage and dry cleaning may seem inconsequential but as one dentist told me, he spends $3000/year on the laundering of coats. It may not seem relevant when you are doing it but these costs can certainly add up to a lot of money and can make a dent in the profits of your practice.

Many factors will contribute to your budget and the benchmarks that you should seek to achieve with each of the line items, including the dental specialty of your practice.

The Levin Group, a consulting firm specializing in dental practices, recommends the following overhead benchmarks by specialty[4]:

Table 3: Overhead benchmarks for dental professions

Specialty	Overhead	Staff salaries	Clinical supplies
General dentistry	60%	20%–25%	6%–8%
Orthodontics	55%	18%–22%	8%–9%
Endodontics	42%	6%–8%	15%–20%
Oral and maxillofacial	45%	15%–18%	10%–15%
Pediatric dentistry	49%	18%–25%	6%–10%
Periodontics	57%	22%–28%	12%–16%
Prosthodontics	60%	23%–30%	8%–10%

Source: internal data

4 https://www.dentaleconomics.com/money/article/16391806/how-does-your-overhead-compare-to-national-averages

Figure 2: Median specialist revenue and overhead

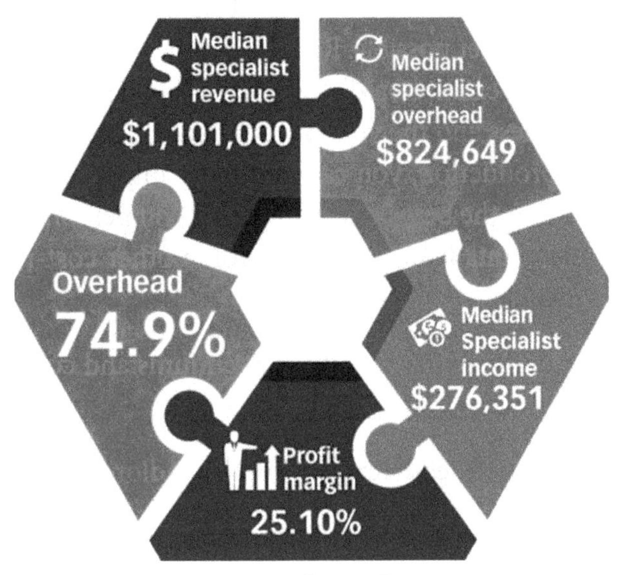

Image courtesy of Dental Economics

Overhead too high?

If you find that in your new practice your overhead expenses are hovering in that 70+% range, it is time to take action. Of course, increasing production, including hygiene production, can decrease overhead percentages against your fixed expenses such as rent and utilities. You should also consider other ways of increasing revenue such as:

- Adjusting fees to be in alignment with national averages
- Working to reduce the number of cancellations and no-show clients
- Increasing how you receive referrals
- Increasing the acceptance of procedures by patients by developing scripts to be used by employees

Aside from trying to increase revenue, it is the responsibility of the owner as well as all staff to always be mindful of cost reductions wherever possible. Reducing costs = reduced overhead percentages. For example, although dental supplies are a necessity to doing business and the volume required will increase with an increase in production, you can and more importantly, should shop around for the best price, comparing competitors and even quantity discounts from suppliers. Some other cost-reducing strategies include:

- Regularly review insurance premiums and coverage for potential savings
- Renegotiate lease terms with the landlord
- Contact suppliers of utilities such as electricity, internet, and telephone to evaluate usage and implement any cost savings programs
- Re-evaluate healthcare costs and benefit packages to economically meet the needs of employees and staff.
- Look for savings in any area that you can. The reduction in expenses increases your profit margins, putting more money in your pocket as the business owner.

The X factor; Marketing

"Good marketing makes the company look smart.
Great marketing makes the customer feel smart."
~ Joe Chernov, VP of Marketing, HubSpot

"People don't buy what you do, they buy why you do it."
~ Simon Sinek, Author, Ted Talk speaker

I have been a part of practices that market heavily and some that don't market at all. Some have an established reputation that naturally draws new patients, others have an ideally placed location, while some expertly use blogs and social media to build their name.

Whatever the approach, marketing will undoubtedly be a key ingredient to your practice's success and is therefore worth taking a closer look at. First, let's review some general data for average marketing costs, then see what some of our colleagues have to say from their experience. We will end with a review of Pareto's Law and how you can apply it to your marketing strategies.

According to researchers in the dental industry, a practice's marketing budget should be between 10% and 12.5% of the revenues the practice owner would like to generate. However, of course, there will be external factors that will play a very important role in this calculation including location, population density, and desired practice growth.

A 2020 survey of how much dental offices spend on marketing[5] monthly reveals:

- 7% — No marketing expenses
- 6% — Under $200
- 9% — $200-500
- 25% — $500-1,000
- 20% — $1,000-2,000
- 12% — $2,000-5,000
- 22% — Over $5,000

5 http://www.thewealthydentist.com/blog/2325/22-of-dentists-spend-over-5k-a-month-on-dental-marketing/

This astonishing number of 22% of dentists spending more than $5K per month on marketing tells us of the important role that marketing plays in bringing in new clients and nurturing the relationship with existing ones.

Unfortunately, for some small or startup offices, the subject of marketing becomes a Catch 22. Because of location, or size, etc., the office does not bring in enough new clients organically, and therefore, there is not enough money in the budget for marketing. On the other hand, if you spend money on marketing, you will bring in new clients and therefore, not have the capacity to see and treat them all in a timely fashion. As you develop your budget, be sure to include some numbers in your budget to start getting your name out there. As you increase production, this number can be adjusted but again the dollar that most practices should shoot for is between 10 and 12.5% of expected revenues dedicated to marketing efforts.

One dentist I spoke to shares his thoughts and motivation for marketing. "While the location is a huge factor in determining where you establish your business, it will also play a major role in how you market it. You need to have something that sets you apart from the others, especially if there are other dentists within a small radius. Maybe it is your personality or offerings or even your marketing and online presence. These can definitely help you to make up the difference in the location or proximity and attract customers to the practice."

As we talked about earlier in Chapter 6 and this practice owner mentioned, location plays a major role in your marketing efforts as well as will impact how much you may need to allocate in your budget for marketing expenses.

Marketing takes on many forms for a dental practice. From billboards and signs to advertising and building an online presence. Which avenue you use to reach your patients will depend on several factors including budget, location, and intent.

An owner of a small practice tells me "there are very few dentists in America and the ones that have very prominent practices really turned social media into a patient-attracting tool." For most offices, social media is supplemental marketing that is there because patients will go on it. But it's not going to actually grab you patients. Very few people have been able to really make social media work as a means of bringing in new patients. That's not to say that we haven't gotten patients from Instagram but it's just a few and far between and they are usually younger, say under 25."

He continues, "Social media marketing is an adjunct to everything else you do. Although Facebook Ads were very popular and inexpensive several years ago, the price has come up. Many offices are doing Facebook Ads and Google AdWords."

If you are a dentist, marketing may not necessarily be your *thing*. While some people are better at social media and marketing than others, you should consider paying someone to manage it for you. This will increase your expenses but depending on your goals of marketing and building your client base, it may be worth it to give it to someone you trust. As technology changes very rapidly, you have to look at marketing from a short-term perspective, reevaluating your plan every 6 months to a year.

Let's look at several things ways that dental practice owners can go about marketing. Of course, every office and location are different and what works for one may not work for another. These are some suggestions that can be used to get you started. However, it is important to note that you must keep your finger on the pulse of what is working for your business versus what is not. If you see that magazine ads are bringing in new patients while radio spots are not, do not waste your money on the radio ads. Do what works best for you, your location, and your practice. Double down on what works, and cut the fat where it's not holding its weight. One office I worked at had such a strong reputation that their only marketing was via patient referrals and word of mouth; no budget for the rest required.... even better!

Digital Marketing

Digital marketing involves creating a strong internet presence through active social media pages, informative blogs, email campaigns, multimedia content such as photos and videos, accurate directory listings, and most importantly your website. Online marketing for dentists is a great way to generate new patients.

In the highly digital world we live in, social media marketing is not just a good way to advertise your services to attract new clients but it has become essential to engaging with your current patients as well.

The amount that you spend on social media can be as broad or narrow a range as you want it to be. Some practices use the free services offered through each platform while others choose to place paid ads spending several thousand dollars per month. Depending upon your location (again), social media can be a very effective tool for acquiring new patients.

Best social media platforms for a dentist:

- Facebook advertising can be used to build deep and trusting relationships with your target audience and display that you are real people who are looking out for their best interests. Engage with new and current patients by:

  - Providing tips for dental hygiene and answering frequently asked questions
  - Offering links to relevant topics and articles
  - Sharing pictures of your staff and other satisfied clients
  - Offering promotions or offers

- YouTube is a great place to show off your office, post patient testimonials, and provide dental tips and suggestions.
- Twitter offers you a way to stimulate trends and followers by using appropriate hashtags for subjects and topics that patients may search for in the industry. For example, #cavityprevention or #teethwhiteningtips. You can quickly and easily engage with prospective patients and show them that you are staying relevant in the industry.
- Instagram is a very useful tool if you want to show off the visual appeal of your practice especially if you are in cosmetic dentistry. Display pictures of satisfied teens after their braces are removed or your older patients showing off their new dentures.

Website

Every business in the world now has to have a website that is appealing, attractive, and provides relevant information. As many patients now search for things they need on their phones, your website needs to be mobile friendly and up to date.

Website design and maintenance prices can range from very inexpensive and basic to highly interactive, elaborate, and therefore, more expensive. However, it is a very effective tool for drawing in new patients if done well.

Your website is where you will create the first impression in the mind of a prospective patient as well as will showcase your specialties and skills that set you apart from the others. When you consider where to get started with a website, you should reach out to a person experienced in web design who understands the ins and outs of reliable web hosting, website design specifically for the dental industry, and who is knowledgeable in dental procedures. In other words, you want someone who is going to help your practice be successful by attracting new clients.

Have you ever searched for something on Google and clicked on the first business that pops up? It came up first because of its website's Search Engine Optimization, its user-friendliness, branding, and customer reviews. These are all important factors when building your website and your brand. On the other hand, some websites will lack appeal and will turn away your interest instantly. Maybe the site was boring, did not provide you with the information that you needed, or did not accurately show that they could meet your needs. This is what you want to avoid because a bad website could be just as harmful to your business as a good one is helpful.

You may be asking what is Search Engine Optimization (SEO)? It is the process of optimizing your website so that it appears in relevant search terms and appearing higher in the search results. It is that thing that puts your website at the top of the list or the ranking when someone searches for a relevant topic or offer. Remember the last time you searched for something? How likely were you to click on that first website on the list?

Things to consider that will boost your SEO.

- Up to date and frequently updated content
- Relevant links
- Site Structure
- Links to Local Directories
- Website Technology such as hosting, domain name, and speed
- Keywords (words that a person looking for your services may enter) – adding the right keywords to your website and content will increase the likelihood that it will show up in a relevant search. For example, if you offer teeth whitening services, be sure that these words are appropriately placed in several areas of your website to enable the algorithms that work behind the scenes to do their job.

Local Dental Directory Listings

It is relatively inexpensive to list your practice in local dental directories, typically $50 - $250 per month and is a very cost-efficient way of getting new patients.

Of course, regardless of the social media method that you choose, or all of them, you must have consistency across all platforms. Be sure that your name, address, and phone number are all correct so that patients can easily find you no matter where they search or which directory they use.

Blogging

Blogging is a great way to drive potential patients to your website. Create original content that may be interesting to someone who is searching for information about a relevant topic. You want to ensure that you post blog articles regularly and consistently share your brand, demonstrate your knowledge, and provide relatable information. For example, how to teach your child to brush his/her teeth, the benefits of flossing, the advantages of dental cosmetics. It would serve no purpose to post blog articles on your website that speak of your favorite restaurant or a movie that you recently saw. Sharing relevant information demonstrates to prospective clients that you are an authority in your specific area of expertise and helps to drive more traffic to your website.

Advertisements (TV, Radio, Billboards, Newspaper, & Mailers)

In many industries, traditional advertising is on the decline and considered to be less effective than online digital marketing strategies. However, if you do consider adding some of these approaches to your budget, be sure to evaluate them for effectivity. You do not want to waste your valuable marketing dollars on something that is not generating revenue for you. These methods can range in pricing from $200 for a local television ad, $500 for local radio, up to $20,000 for a billboard. Newspaper ads can run anywhere between $700 and $15,000 and direct mail advertising will cost several thousand dollars depending upon the size of your demographic.

Online Reviews

No matter what type of marketing you do, even if you receive referrals by word of mouth, it is very important that you obtain a customer review. Positive feedback will greatly improve your chances of persuading a person who is in the market for a new dentist if they read something that a current patient has written about your practice. Do you value reviews yourself? Whether I am looking to buy a new car, a used piece of equipment, or got to a new restaurant, I always read the reviews first.

Online reviews also help to improve your SEO since online search engines typically direct people to businesses that have higher ratings and many reviews. There are several ways to obtain reviews many of which are completely free.

First and foremost, ask your patients to go to your website after they leave your office and post a review. You can send them a follow-up email after their appointment to make sure that they were satisfied with your services as well as to ask them to complete a review.

Studies show that nearly 90% of consumers utilize reviews to help them in their purchasing decisions. This can work against you as well if you have dissatisfied clients so you always want to ensure that you are meeting the needs of your patients. Happy patients equal more new patients.

Reputation Management software is also available to alert you when new reviews are posted. For example, Google Reviews sends an email each time a new review is posted about your practice.

Pareto's Law

Pareto's Law, otherwise known as the 80/20 rule, can be applied to any area of your life and in fact, you want to use it to review your marketing approach to see how you can efficiently and effectively manage your marketing budget.

In terms of dental marketing, you want 80% of your revenue to come from 20% of your clients; 80% of your results from 20% of your effort; 80% of your new clients from 20% of your budget. So, when you look at those things that generate the most bang for your buck when it comes to your marketing strategy, carefully look at those things that give you 80% of your desired result from only 20% of your effort/time/money.

One of the big questions that dentists new to the business of practice ownership have is "how many new patients should you bring in per month?" While it may be a key indicator of whether your marketing efforts are working, there are many factors to consider. Again, location will play a major role in your ability to attract new patients. Are there other dental practices within a 3 to 5-mile radius? How long have you been in business? Did you purchase an existing practice and therefore already have an established base of clients?

One dental colleague of mine told me that in his practice which has been around for several years, he averages 30 new patients per month but that has fluctuated from when he started to when the practice became established. Thus, a clinician shouldn't be fixated on a specific number because the needs of each practice can vary greatly. To determine how many new patients you will need to earn the profit that you are looking for, you will need to do your research. As discussed in Chapter 6, you will need to have a firm understanding of the demographics where the practice is located, know how many other dental practices you are competing against, as well as the amount of money that you are willing and able to spend on marketing, social media, etc.

PS - This being a section that mentions marketing, it only makes sense to take some space to market our website as well. The plan is to build a community of members like yourselves who are eager to learn more about topics we have discussed in this book and other unaddressed needs within the dental profession.

On our site, you will find a mentorship program that will connect you with other colleagues who want to share their expertise in a few specific topics and provide 1 on 1 direct mentorship to show you the ropes. We are bringing the answers to you directly from experienced clinicians all on *your schedules*. Not too shabby! As great as Facebook groups and study clubs are, having a dedicated colleague to personally work with you is a unique asset worth investing in. The difference it can make on your practice and your overall career are significant. Plus, sponsor perks and other relevant content you will want to know about. So, check us out and join our community!

www.fsg4dentists.com

8

A Word about Insurance

"I told my dentist my teeth are going yellow. He told me to wear a brown tie"
~ Rodney Dangerfield, Famous Comedian

"My dentist has bad breath... Why every time he smokes he blows onion rings"
~ Rodney Dangerfield, Famous Comedian

It's worth making mention of insurance, as unfortunately, it has slowly taken center stage, not only in the running of a dental practice but more importantly, in the decision-making process of every patient. Also, the fees insurance companies "cover" and compensate often result in a significantly smaller profit for you and your practice.

According to a survey published by the Harvard Business Review, approximately 23 percent of Americans or 74 million people in the U.S. do not have dental coverage and more than one-third of American adults haven't seen a dental professional in the past year[6]. Why not? Reportedly, 40 % said that it was because of cost.

Let's briefly discuss some general points on each topic of importance you will come across.

- To take or not to take?
- Is accepting insurance plans for your practice even worth doing? Why cut yourself out of the extra profits if you don't have to? The short answer, according to popular demand and studies, is yes.

Patients often make their initial decision on whether or not they will consider coming to your office based on whether or not you accept their plan; ask them the specific details of what their plan even covers, and they have no clue. The only thing that matters is that they feel "covered" by your practice accepting their specific carrier. Considering dropping their carrier, or all carriers for that matter is a significant gamble you have to plan and prepare for well in advance.

I know of two offices who used to take insurances and decided to no longer accept insurance plans; the thinking behind this approach is that the remaining patients will be sufficient enough to make up the difference, paying at higher rates instead of the normal fees, which would offset any losses the practice would suffer from patients who chose to leave since their plan was no longer accepted. Further, the hope is that some patients could be convinced that staying and paying the full fee is beneficial to them compared to leaving the office, either from office loyalty, relationships, or because they promise better "quality" work; it's a plan they have to justify.

---

6 https://www.coloniallife.com/employer-resource-center/2018/april/the-surprising-truth-about-dental-insurance

In both cases, the practices instantly lost a significant percentage of their patients and over time were not able to sustain the loss of income from this approach. This doesn't mean it can't be done, but if that is your goal, then you really need to make a long-term plan, implement things slowly and very gradually, and spend a significant amount of time on patient education. Some offices will also create their own "in-house" insurance plan, which can work as well, but again requires planning and preparation.

Choosing insurance plans to accept

Ok, I will accept insurance. Which plans should I take?

This is another good question and the answers vary.

There are many heavyweight players that are used nationwide such as Blue Cross, Cigna, and MetLife among others. But depending on what region/state you work in, certain smaller plans are also available which can often provide competing, and maybe even better, benefits. Thus, while you almost can't ignore the big carriers, it's worth making sure you consider some of the lesser-known ones as well. Think about it. When trying to purchase your practice and/or obtain a home loan, oftentimes, it's the smaller banks that offer the best rates, not the giants like Bank of America (sorry BofA).

According to Investopedia, the top-rated plans for 2020[7] include:

Best Dental Insurance Providers of 2020

- Cigna: Best Overall
- Renaissance Dental: Runner-Up, Best Overall

---

7 https://www.investopedia.com/best-dental-insurance-4843282

- Spirit Dental: Best for No Waiting Periods
- Humana Dental Insurance: Best Value
- UnitedHealthOne Dental Insurance: Best for Families
- Physicians Mutual: Best for Seniors
- Delta Dental: Best for Orthodontics

Check out their link for more in-depth details of each plan at https://www.investopedia.com/best-dental-insurance-4843282

Some due diligence and research on your end can determine what percentage of your patient pool uses which insurance plan. This is a necessary step as you can't afford to cut away a plan that 80% of your patients potentially use! Yes, if their fees are noticeably worse than other plans, you can certainly make a gradual effort in educating your patients about this and planning for a gradual shift away from one plan toward others. But this takes time and should be a long-term goal at best. Often, the hassle and work required may not be worth the intended reward.

Specialist vs. Regular Fees

Note that insurance companies compensate differently if you are a specialist. This is critical to know; if your office is submitting your work as a general dentist when you are a specialist, then your compensation is being limited and the office collection as well. No Bueno! At the same time, this is something for owners thinking about having a multi-specialty practice to consider as well. Yes, you could do that endo, extraction, or implant. But if the compensation you will receive (and your practice receives) is less, and requires you doing the extra work and taking on the extra liability, it may be worth your while to have a specialist. This way you can see a patient of your own during the same allotted time, earn on that while earning 50% on work your specialist is doing without ever having to lift a finger. Not a bad deal!

Submitting Considerations and Timing

The only thing worse than having to deal with insurance is forgetting to submit the claims and not being compensated to begin with. This is where your office manager and staff come into play. It's a massive undertaking to keep tabs on insurance claims and to regularly submit, check the status, and make sure you are being properly and fully compensated. A good staff will make or break your practice on this facet alone. It's easy for claims to stack up, and often colleagues of mine spend "off" days coming in just to dedicate time for this process.

As a clinician, you can't collect your pay on what hasn't been collected. So, you must check on insurance as well as monitor the overall collection rate of your office. As we mentioned elsewhere in the book, you want to make sure your office collection is at least 85% and above, ideally in the 95% and above range.

Equally as important and annoying is that the actual claims processing time takes weeks. Plan accordingly and know that when you first sign up for an insurance plan through the credentialing process that alone can take weeks to sometimes even months to fully setup. In other words, the money will be even slower to roll in. Thus, you might begin doing many procedures at a new office and be extremely productive yet receive paychecks at a fraction of the amount you expected. Therefore, the sooner you can begin the credentialing process, the better.

If you have signed a contract with a practice and are set to start a few months later, start and complete the credentialing process immediately so that once you begin, you can already be set up and avoid the massive lag time for your claims and payment.

Getting Creative

One way to hedge your bets if you are anti-insurance but don't want to lose your patients is to offer an in-house insurance plan of your own. I have seen this done in some practices and it can be effective but will require stellar communication and a solid relationship with your patients. Springing this idea as a new clinician or on new patients will make this far more challenging, but the rewards can be there.

For starters, insurance plans don't offer much insurance! The coverage amounts are tiny, and it often takes one procedure to already exceed the yearly amount. Second, insurance coverage is often based on "pre-existing conditions" and/or other conditions like "neighboring teeth present" or "hasn't had a similar procedure in the same quadrant for 4 years". Thus, you will have cases where patients want treatment, but their specific plan won't cover them for some ridiculous reason or other, and then it becomes a hassle and patients will delay treatment.

Thus, some practices offer in-house plans where they offer similar or more yearly money benefits without the conditions. You can dictate the amount of benefit you want to offer along with the terms. Yes, this is more work for your office to manage, but again, in many cases, this can save you quite a bit of hassle, increase case acceptance, and provide an alternative plan to existing insurance which you can then use to slowly but surely wiggle your way out of the vice grip the insurance companies have us in. You could also create a payment plan within the insurance plan itself, so it can act as an alternative to traditional insurance and payment plans such as Care Credit.

The bottom line is that insurance and insurance companies are a massive part of any dental practice business. The more efficiently you can manage the paperwork process and communication with your patients the better. Unfortunately, over the past decade, insurance companies have started to make big dents in the medical field and have slowly but surely similarly crept into the dental world. Delta Dental of Massachusetts cut much of its fee schedule over the past two years, resulting in compensation for many procedures at 30% the prior amount. This means you have to work that much harder to make up the difference.

That being said, MA is far better off in terms of compensation compared to other states like NY or AZ to name a few. One friend in AZ was being compensated just $16 for each molar extraction he was doing; certainly not a winning formula. Educate yourself on your state's plans, carriers, compensation, and your current or prospective patient base distribution of plans and take it from there. Just another factor to consider.

9

Partners, Associates and Never Leaving the House

"Do not go where the path may lead,
go instead where there is no path and leave a trail."
~ Ralph Waldo Emerson, famous American poet

"Alone we can do so little; together we can do so much."
~ Helen Keller - American author and activist;
first deaf/blind person to earn a BA degree

Growing up my two favorite sports were basketball and tennis; two totally different sports in every sense. Basketball was a team game; without good teammates and good coaching, it's hard to win. Tennis on the other hand has no coaching, no time outs, and no one to sub in for you when you aren't playing well. Even if you played doubles (which given my basketball affinity was what

I preferred) it was still up to you and your partner to figure things out. If you had to choose between them, which one do you prefer?

Dental ownership is certainly not a sport, but depending on how you want to practice, you can make it a partnership or go it alone. Each has its pros and cons; I've seen many colleagues have tremendous success with a partner and also seen some that were a disaster and literally ended friendships. I've also seen some very successful solo practice owners who believe staying solo was the smartest thing they ever did, while some have said they wished they had a partner instead.

As is the case with most topics in this book, there isn't a single winning formula. Much of it comes down to your long-term goals, the lifestyle you want to live, and your personality. For some, it's solely a business move. Either way, the thought will cross your mind many times throughout your career, so I want to break down some of the potential pros and cons of having a partnership and share some advice from a few friends who have tried both approaches.

According to most of the dentists that I interviewed, the question of whether to partner or not is a very individual decision and will depend on many factors including your personality, the location, and the size.

My friend Brendan shares his perspective on having a partner which he knows may not be a general consensus but may help look at the pros and cons of partnership.

> "I wanted a partner because I didn't want to do everything by myself. I specifically didn't want to do the marketing, budgeting, forecasting. I don't enjoy doing them. So, if I can have a partner who likes doing those things or that can help with those things,

> it makes sense. But the flip side of that is that having a partner is very hard. I think the best partners are partners that are not friends. They are just colleagues and business partners. That way you take a friendship level out of it because it is just purely business. I am not friends with my business partner. We are business partners. That is where the line goes."

For many dental practices, this type of partnership works very well. You respect each other and understand where each of you has your strengths and weaknesses. There is no emotion involved in it; just business.

Now friends like him and others I know can say this very firmly and clearly because they have personally experienced the other side; in these cases, the grass was certainly not greener! Whether it be close friends, prior classmates, and even family relatives, I've seen how mixing personal relationships into business more often than not leads to trouble. Again, as with everything in life, there are exceptions, and given the right combination, you can flourish in any situation. But ask around enough and the consensus on this topic is pretty clear: don't mix the two!

Associate

When it comes to the timing of bringing on an associate dentist or a partner, this again is a very individual decision. Many dentists prefer to work alone but if you are looking for scalability, you certainly cannot be all things to all people. You cannot practice dentistry, meeting with all patients, and manage the daily ins and outs of the business. At some point, if you are looking to grow, you may have to consider bringing on an associate. In other words, bring another dentist into the practice.

For recent graduates, becoming an associate as an established practice is highly recommended. You more than likely are coming out with a large amount of debt and very little experience. It is going to be very difficult to manage your student loans, take on a practice loan, try to learn dentistry, and negotiate the perils of opening a practice. In the opinion of most dentists I spoke to, becoming an associate dentist first and learning the ropes is the way to go before jumping into practice ownership.

But for the practice owner who is looking to hire an associate, when is the right time and what do you look for in hiring a dentist?

A key factor to note is that an associate relationship must work for both parties. For most graduates, the motivation is two-fold; high student loan debt and "try before you buy". In other words, a recent graduate from dental school cannot get a loan yet due to high student loans, and most importantly, they want to understand what it means and takes to own a dental practice before they jump in with both feet.

If you are looking to hire an associate, what is your motivation? Is it to relieve the excessive patient load, is it to build patient flow for future buy-in as a partner, or are you planning for retirement? Some hiring dentists have personal interests, such as wanting to provide coverage for when they cannot be in the office or hopes that the new dentist will grow their practice.

Potential pitfalls whether you are looking to hire or become an associate

While the intentions of both parties are usually good, things can still turn sour if communication is not effective. Some of the more common reasons for the relationship not to work include incompatible philosophies of practice, inability to support an additional dentist, unrealistic expectations for time, compensation, or both, and owner dentist unwillingness to relinquish control.

Potential fixes

At the end of the day, the greatest fix is a written contract. As in every relationship, we are all the most open-minded in the beginning. Putting the agreement in writing maximizes the honeymoon period and minimizes the chance of future misunderstanding and disagreement.

Compensation

A key point of interest is the compensation of an associate. Again, whether you are considering joining an existing dental practice or hiring an associate, is a critical part of the conversation and decision to hire.

- Paid on percentage: Love it or hate it, the current typical range for compensation is 25% to 35% of the associate's production or collection. Many dentists also get minimum guaranteed annual compensation. This is a mutually beneficial scenario for both the associate and the owning dentist, as there is an incentive for the associate to produce. It also allows the owning dentist the ability to plan financially for the associate's salary.

- Many times, the issue of who should pay the lab bill presents itself in this compensation method. A simple way to solve this is to have the bills removed from the production or collection figures before the final compensation being calculated.

- Paid on salary: Another common approach, salaries can be hourly, daily, or on monthly base pay. Many young dentists like the security of salary-based compensation. This allows for financial planning and the security of knowing how much money to budget. With the national average student loan debt being $287,331, the payment plans terrify many students and make the prospect of a guaranteed salary very appealing. On the other hand, you usually do not make as much money with this compensation plan. Consider if you can handle the risk of having a bad month, or if you are willing to give up the potential earnings of percentage-based compensation for the security of a salary.

- Paid per diem: More commonly found for independent contractors/specialists, but still an option for all, is to pay per diem. This arrangement guarantees an established payment amount for the day(s) you work no matter what. You may see 20 patients, or maybe have many cancelations and only treat 3; regardless, you will have a guaranteed income for that day as long as you are scheduled and present in the office. This provides further reassurance and flexibility for the practitioner, especially for an associate who is early in their career, as they know they will earn something for the day and can focus more on the cases and less on the production amount. It is in some ways a variation of a salary, but many DSO/corporations offer this form of payment for their specialists rather than a salary. In some cases, despite the per diem guarantee, if you produce more than your daily cut in a given day you will be able to earn the higher of the two amounts; in other cases, that number is fixed no matter what and balances itself out over a year. A great example of per diem payment is for an ortho associate who is seeing 60 patients/day; keeping track of the payment and insurances can be a nightmare, so offering the fixed per diem rate is the way to go.

- Paid on a draw: While a less common method of earning, being paid on a draw means being paid expected future earnings. This can also be explained as a loan against projected income. If the associate's percentage collection or production is less than the agreed amount of the salary, the office will cover the difference in the associate's pay. The net of what the associate has earned minus what the associate has been paid will then be settled as the end of a set amount of time. In this scenario, the associate can owe the owning dentist money at different points in time.

In the end, there are many important considerations when it comes to answering the question of whether you can make an associate relationship work. **Know your why**. **Know your counterpart's why**. **Build a contract** on the front end that maximizes everyone's success and minimizes everyone's risk. And don't forget the **compensation**. It may be the dirty little secret no one wants to talk about, but it's a deal maker or a deal-breaker.

Aside from the financial reason for becoming an associate right after graduation, it can allow a new dentist to grow and learn before jumping in. Developing a relationship in which you can learn and grow from a seasoned practice owner may put you in a better position moving forward to either become a partner or purchase your own practice in the future. As an associate, you have the advantage of having a full-time mentor, assuming that the owner is willing to share the business side of practice ownership as well.

One dental colleague who I spoke with started her career as an associate, spent several years learning as much as she could, and then opened her own practice. At first, she did not think that she would ever hire an associate dentist to work with her. Now realizing how much work practice ownership is, she will consider hiring an associate in the future just to reduce the amount of work for herself. Ownership changed her perspective.

Another close friend who is an orthodontist and partner in an ortho practice in Montreal speaks very highly of the benefits of being involved in a partnership. In his experience, teaming up as a partner in practice provides several key benefits:

- The office never closes! You can each plan your vacations and time off around each other's schedule without disrupting regular office hours. This also means that there will always be revenue coming in at all times which for a partnership is ideal since profits are shared. Now you can travel in relative peace knowing someone is there to hold the fort until you return. Not a bad business model!

- He also mentions the benefit of having a colleague in-house to discuss cases, treatment plan options, and to bounce ideas off of. In that sense, his practice acts as its own mini-study club and also helps prevent the boredom of being on your own all day.

To this, I know my sister can also attest. Having had her own private practice for many years, she had no option of having another dentist work if she wanted to take time off, something that affects all solo practice owners. Even if you keep the office open for hygiene, you are always concerned if things are running smoothly while you are away, or are getting bombarded with calls by your front desk staff with questions and issues. Not much of a vacation!

Also, whatever free time existed between patients was spent in her back-office sorting through paperwork and doing things on her own, which once you are 10 to 15 years into your career, can start getting old really quickly! So, although we discuss and warn of some of the potential risks and pitfalls of having a partner, done correctly and with the right match, it can become a significant benefit for your career!

Lastly, it is important to note that just because you have an opinion about associateship, partnership, or ownership TODAY, it does not mean that your perspective may not change throughout various times in your career and life. During each stage of your dental career, it may be more beneficial to engage in one type of relationship or another depending upon the needs of your practice, your personal needs as well as desire to expand or even retire. Thus, things will certainly evolve with time, and no decision today has to be a permanent one for your entire career.

Termination

As important as the conversation about hiring an associate is, there are also certain things to keep in mind if the relationship does not work out and you have to terminate an associate. Having to tell someone that they are terminated is never a fun or easy task and should not be taken lightly. This is someone's livelihood that you are talking about, the way that they feed their families. Of course, there are many reasons that you may have to terminate/fire an employee or associate including disregard for your code of conduct, poor performance or behavior, disciplinary, or lack of work (thank you COVID-19).

This is where having a Human Resources handbook will be especially important and will be used as your guide to handle or avoid any employment disputes and potential lawsuits.

There are some rules and guidelines that you should consider to keep yourself and your practice out of hot water:

- Document any problems or issues with the employee as they occur. The process for reprimanding an employee should be well-documented in the handbook (i.e. number of written warnings before action is taken).
- This is a private matter between you and the employee. It should not be discussed with other associates or employees.
- During the actual conversation to terminate employment, be very clear and succinct. If you have been documenting any issues along the way, it should be evident why you are taking action.
- You are looking out for the best interest of your practice so do not apologize, blame, or be defensive.
- Keep the conversation as positive as possible and wish the person well.
- Pay the employee immediately for any monies owed and escort the associate to collect their belongings. Be sure to collect any keys or property of the practice before they leave.

As difficult as the process of termination is, it is a part of practice ownership and therefore worth mentioning.

Double Dipping: Owning your practice and the real estate (and maybe even living there!)

"Ninety percent of all millionaires become so through owning real estate"
~ Andrew Carnegie - American steel magnate and millionaire

Chances are that very few of us will be in the position to buy a practice along with the corresponding property itself right out of the gate, but that doesn't mean it can't become a possibility one day in the future there or a different location.

Benefits of owning property

Dental practices that rent or lease property typically make many improvements to the office space, ultimately making the property more appealing for the landlord. Paying rent does not build up any equity for you nor does it have the same tax deductions as property ownership. To plan for your retirement and financial future, you may want to consider owning the property where your dental practice is located.

Understandably, this is a major decision and commitment to your practice and personal financial planning.

- Paying a mortgage payment creates equity as you pay down the debt
- You have control over the property, external signage for marketing and promotion
- Depending on the size of the space required for the dental practice, you may be able to rent out additional space, bringing in an additional stream of income, helping to pay down the mortgage even faster.

- When you decide to retire, you can determine how you want the property to be handled – as part of the sale or as a rental agreement.

The decision to purchase or lease depends greatly on where in the life cycle are you in your dental career.

- Recent graduate. If you are just coming out of dental school, overwhelmed and burdened by student loans, this is probably not the time to consider investing in property. Especially if you are starting your own practice, having to build your reputation and practice revenue, adding the expense of a mortgage may not be in your best interest.
- Mid-career. This may be the perfect time and opportunity to consider purchasing property for your dental practice. As mentioned earlier, it is never too early to begin thinking about your retirement and office property may be just the bump that your retirement portfolio needs.
- Late-career. If you have owned your practice for many years and are considering selling at some point in the next 5 to 10 years, owning commercial property may be an investment in your future. You may be able to sell it to the future owner of the practice or lease it under the purchase agreement, guaranteeing a lifetime of income during your retirement.

These decisions are all very valuable and important to your future as a dentist and should not be taken lightly. Be sure to consult with your financial advisor and accountant to determine what is best for you at each stage of your career.

Considerations for the buy or lease question

As with any other financial decision, there are many factors to consider which again should be discussed with your team of trusted advisors.

- Capital investment is a good thing if you have the capital to spare. Do not burden yourself with additional debt if it will place additional strain and drain on your finances.
- Cash liquidity. Purchasing a commercial building ties up cash. Depending upon where you are in the life cycle discussed earlier, consider how liquid you need or want your money to be.
- As the owner of the property, all repairs and maintenance will fall on you. Aside from managing your dental practice, you will have to take into consideration building management and tenant obligations such as rent collection, increases, and budgeting for repairs and maintenance.
- For tax and liability purposes, it is better to own the property through a separate legal entity. Again, be sure to seek legal and financial counsel on this as well as consider the type of corporate organization as was discussed in Chapter 3.

As you can see, there are many benefits to owning the building where your dental practice is. In fact, you may consider even purchasing a building with enough space to not only house your practice but where you can live as well. Why not kill two birds with one stone! The benefits in this scenario far outweigh the repairs, maintenance, and expenses associated with commercial property ownership. However, I cannot reiterate enough that you must seek the advice and counsel of your financial advisor, accountant, and attorney before deciding to purchase commercial property.

PART FOUR

Facing your biggest fears...or a Pandemic

10

The Gut Punch

"Everyone has a plan until they get punched in the face"
~ Mike Tyson, former boxing Heavyweight Champion of the world

"It's not whether you get knocked down. It's whether you get back up"
~ Vince Lombardi, Hall of Fame, Green Bay Packers

Coronavirus pandemic aside, there is no bigger fear for every dental professional than having a lawsuit or complaint filed against them. The process is stressful and will make you question why you ever bothered entering the profession. Chances are at some point in your career you will come across this situation no matter how great a dentist you are.

In New Zealand, where I have lectured several years in a row for my EarAid hearing protection product (which if you haven't heard of before you should seriously consider and look into on our website www.fsg4dentists.com, bias aside), the government has a built-in fund in place specifically for such conflicts; the cases are heard and any payment, if determined necessary comes from this government, allotted fund. No-fuss, no trials, no suing and days in court or in front of a board, and therefore no risk to lose your license and end your career…simple.

Unfortunately, in our sue-happy culture, such a program doesn't exist. Understanding how the process works and preparing yourself to minimize any risks if it ever occurs is your best bet, so lets' review the process and provide some tips to prepare you.

Lawsuits in Dentistry

I am sure that you have heard the rumblings within the dental industry. It is very common for dentists to be afraid of being sued during their careers and with good reason. Unfortunately, there is a wide range of negative consequences that result from a lawsuit of any kind including financial implications, negative reputation, along with mental, physical, and emotional stress.

As in a medical practice, a lawsuit against a dentist falls under the category of Malpractice and may arise from a variety of procedures or reasons.

- Complications with tooth extractions, bridges, root canals and crowns
- Complications due to anesthesia
- Failure to diagnose oral diseases or cancers
- Oral nerve damage
- Unexpected reactions to Novocain
- Infections

- Wrongful Death (although this is highly unlikely in a dental practice, unfortunately, things happen)

The necessity and requirement for malpractice insurance were discussed in Chapter 4 so I will not dwell on it further in this chapter. I do want to talk about the other types of challenges that you as a dental practice owner could face that could really direct a punch to the gut.

Dental Board Complaints

The Dental Board is the regulatory department that regulates the licensing of dentists and the operation of dental practices.

Unfortunately, patients who believe that they have been the victim of some wrong, they may file a complaint with the local dental board. For example, complaints may include gross negligence, illegal activities, the licensing or qualifications of the dentist, and the use of dangerous or controlled substances.

All claims filed with the Dental Board must be followed by a thorough investigation to substantiated the validity of the claim. Not only could this process be lengthy but it is an inconvenience for the practice and the patient. If it is determined that the practice is in fact guilty of the infraction, it has the authority to take disciplinary action against the dentist and/or dental practice including fines, revocation of dental license, suspension from practicing, and public notice of the action.

Due to the serious nature of the dental board complaint and its ramifications on your finances and future business, it is highly recommended that you follow best practices as deemed by the dental board.

Insurance Provider Audits

Included in the contract of the dental insurance policies (as discussed in chapter 4), there will be the contractual obligation and requirement to conduct regular audits of best practices, insurance, and billing patterns. Insurance carriers want to ensure that the practice meeting is meeting all state and local requirements as well as not engaging in any fraudulent or potentially harmful activities.

Audits can be messy and complicated if your practice is not following established guidelines. This is where many of the subjects that we have been discussing throughout this book conjoin. As a practice owner, you must ensure the safety of your patients, employees, property, and take financial responsibility for all of it. Manuals, policies, procedures, software, and record-keeping all come in to play when that auditor walks in the door to evaluate or investigate your practice.

An audit takes a significant amount of time and can jeopardize your practice and livelihood if not taken seriously. The best way to ensure the security of your business and income is to comply with all regulations and policies and have a system of proper record-keeping and accountability. Hopefully, you have received the proper information in the previous chapters to guide you as to what is required and how to manage your practice to avoid a negative outcome from an audit.

Although it is required, an audit does not have a negative outcome or even be difficult as long as you have your ducks in a row.

Employment Lawsuits

The very fact that you have employees opens up the possibility of employee grievances and disputes. A thorough a complete employee handbook and the advice of a Human Resource professional can significantly reduce the possibility of an employee filing a lawsuit against you, someone on your team, or the practice itself. Employment lawsuits can range from wage disputes to sexual harassment to gender, age, or racial discrimination, many of which can be taken to the Federal level for resolution if deemed necessary.

Partnership Disputes

As I discussed earlier, a partnership is hard work and it is an individual decision whether it is right for you and your practice. If you do choose to partner with someone in your dental practice, it is imperative that not only do you do your research in advance but you have the appropriate contract in place before beginning the relationship. Partnership disputes can make or break a dental practice.

Disputes among partners may involve finances, responsibilities, accountability, or liabilities and can play a major role in lawsuits, audits, and employee grievances if not handled or managed properly. Therefore, the reason and importance of carefully selecting someone to go into partnership with as well as having a contractual agreement established and agreed upon by both parties.

If you are considering bringing on a partner, be sure to consult with a dental practice attorney who is familiar with the ins and outs of a dental practice. Save yourself the headache and trouble of having to dissolve a practice or partnership later on because of the lack of proper planning upfront.

State Dental Board

As the local dental board is commissioned to monitor the activities of a dentist and dental practice, the State Dental Board's responsibility is to protect dental patients in accordance with the Dental Practice Act. Local licensing boards may elect to bring incidents of unprofessional conduct, incompetence, and gross negligence to the attention of the State Dental Board for further disciplinary or even criminal action.

Each of these challenges can deliver a debilitating blow to you and your dental practice and unfortunately for some may shut down a dental practice completely. It is critical that you as pursue your career in dentistry that you abide by the rules and regulations of the various organizations, authorities, and groups to ensure the longevity and success of your business and career.

To ensure that you are following generally accepted dental practices, be sure to include some of the following forms and documents as part of your operational and patient procedures:

- Patient forms including Informed Consent, Treatment Plan Consent or Refusal, HIPAA and Patient Health History Form
- Human Resource forms including Clinician Fitness Verification, Credentialing and Privileging, Performance Evaluations, Employment Agreements, and Incident Form
- Guidelines and requirements for staff and associates should also be clearly written and explained to ensure that everyone on your staff is aware of and is following best practices as deemed by the dental board as well as of the practice. These documents should include Quality Control, Risk Assessment Forms, and Operational Procedures.

Personal Note:

I don't know anyone amongst my group of dental school colleagues who have not had to deal with some form of complaint during their career. It seems like it's an inevitable occurrence no matter what you do and how careful you are. All you can do is your best, document, and have a clear conscience.

I am no different in this regard. In a decade of practicing, I have had two instances where a complaint was considered, but in the end, dropped. One occurred in just my first year out which made it even scarier. The irony in both cases is that I had gone above and beyond the norm to help these individuals in their situations before there was ever an "issue."

One claimed to have complications understanding English, leading to miscommunication, confusion over her treatment plan options, and confusion over the treatment given itself. The only thing was that my assistant just happened to be from the same country, spoke the language fluently, and reviewed every step in *both* languages, even providing detailed instructions in writing and following up via phone every step of the way as an additional courtesy. No matter...this individual figured they could file a complaint and ultimately get her money back which is what many times is what it's all about.

Thanks to our solid documentation, and the fact that we did every step with her in two languages (the best part was that her English was just fine when it needed to be), there was no case. That didn't stop me from having to contact my malpractice insurance provider, put in a claim, go through interviews, review all case notes, etc. It was a hassle but again, that's why we pay for malpractice insurance!

Unfortunately, it doesn't take much to file a complaint, but yet it requires a lot of time and lost sleep often to clear things up. But again, if you did nothing wrong, if you documented well, and if you have more than one source to confirm your story, things will work themselves out. For this reason, it's always important to have someone else in the room with you whenever you do a consult and especially when dealing with a difficult or complaining patient. Having your assistant or manager there gives a second source of validity to your side and makes it harder to refute.

In another classic instance I experienced, a patient had extraction complications and complained of severe, debilitating pain. They claimed that the material we used and put into the socket (a collagen plug) was the cause of the pain, that it was coming out creating the pain and making it even worse. This person also happened to be a lawyer, which just doubled the threats and tough-guy rhetoric. The complaints being made in her story didn't make any sense, and at every step of the post-op we reviewed, the patient was insistent that she was following things to the finest detail.

The patient came in for a follow-up. After drafting letters to us threatening a lawsuit, she came in with her son for added effect. While she sat in the waiting room, the staff noticed she was downing her giant Dunkin Donuts iced coffee with a ***STRAW.*** Not just a random sip, but the entire iced coffee, just sucking away on that straw. Long story short, a brief explanation, and exchange (with her son in the room for added effect, of course) ended that issue before it ever reached a complaint stage. You just never know…

In regards to employee disputes, this has also been quite an interesting time during the pandemic. Employees have been earning more money by staying home and collecting unemployment in most cases than coming back to work, which has created an interesting situation for most practices and owners alike. I know multiple friends who have been dealing with hygienists, front office staff, and back-office assistants who are refusing to come back, have quit, or in most cases, want to return a few weeks later. The results have added even further strain on the owners trying to restart their businesses.

One thing that has helped them each is having clear communication with *all* staff from the start, maintaining that communication throughout the crisis, and making the options and expectations clear. Each owner has made their staff aware of the likely need to let them go if they choose to not return when reopened, as the office cannot survive without its staff. Having clean communication, documentation, and very clear language in your employment contracts, and any updated Covid-19 paperwork and employee return forms will be vital to protect your practice and minimize risk. Just another thing for owners to deal with it!

11

Worst-case scenarios

"Success is not final, failure is not fatal; it is the courage to continue that counts"
~ Winston Churchill, British Prime Minister WWII

Hopefully, by this point in the book, you are already feeling better prepared to flourish in your career. Your student loans are under a controlled schedule based on your plan, you have negotiated a fair contract with the practice you joined, you have the right insurance plans in place and some money set aside for your future, and as a new owner, you have balanced your overhead with your ambitious goals of building your brand.

That being said, sometimes even our best efforts don't work out as we want them to; life throws us a curveball we can't hit and we strike out, or mother nature enters the equation with different plans of her own. Maybe even a global pandemic occurs.

The worst-case scenarios can jeopardize all our dreams, but they aren't always impossible to recover from. Let's look at several scenarios that may appear devastating if they are not fully understood.

Bankruptcy

If you find yourself in a desperate financial position for whatever reason, bankruptcy may be an option. It does not eliminate student loans, taxes, child support or alimony so carefully consider this if you are considering filing for bankruptcy. As mentioned several times already, be sure to consult with your financial advisor or accountant to determine your best course of action. Let's look at several types of bankruptcy so that if you do need to go that route, you are informed and knowledgeable about each of the options.

- Chapter 7 Bankruptcy, also known as "straight bankruptcy," is the common term that people use when considering eliminating all debt. Under this type of bankruptcy, the court will order the sale of all assets to pay the outstanding debt excluding student loans, child support, etc. So, if your student loans are weighing you down, take filing Chapter 7 bankruptcy off the table). Certain assets are exempt from the sale including cars, work-related tools, and basic household furnishings).

  Before considering filing Chapter 7, it is important that you clearly understand the ramifications.

  - Sale of all property including real estate, jewelry, antique furnishings, etc.
  - Dissolution of business assets

  - Negative impact on credit score and creditworthiness for up to 10 years

- Chapter 13 Bankruptcy allows you to keep property while agreeing to partially or completely repay the debt over a three to five-year period. The debt is discharged after this time even if the debt has not been paid in full. While retaining some of your assets, Chapter 13 allows you to repay some of your debt and negatively impacts your credit score for only seven years.

The decision to file Chapter 7 or Chapter 13 Bankruptcy will be in large part defined by your assets and income level. If you in fact have enough money to repay the debt, a court may find it more appropriate to file Chapter 13, especially if home foreclosure is to be avoided.

Alternatives to filing Bankruptcy

Bankruptcy is just one option for rectifying your debt dilemma. Bankruptcy has very serious financial ramifications that will follow you for years to come. While most other options will also impact your credit score and creditworthiness for the foreseeable future, the following are certainly the lesser of two evils:

- Debt consolidation loan
- Debt management plan
- Negotiate with current creditors to come up with a solution that will be equitable to both parties. Of course, they do not want to see you default on your loan which would mean that they would not get paid at all.

Criminal Charges

There is one situation that could derail your dental career and which should be avoided at all costs. Criminal charges! While no one wants to be disciplined for any type of infraction or run into trouble with the law, the Dental Board take certain things very seriously and is willing to suspend or revoke a dentist's license if a dentist is brought up on several charges. For example, possession of a forged instrument, receiving stolen property, improper rebating, burglary, crimes involving drugs or alcohol, prescription fraud, practicing under the influence of or possession of controlled substances, driving under the influence, assault with a deadly weapon, and a lewd act with a child.

Although disciplinary action by the dental board varies by state, the state of California has several levels of disciplining a dentist based on criminal convictions that are "substantially related" to the qualifications, functions, or duties of a dentist or dental assistant and may include:

- Placing the licensee on probation
- Suspending or revoking the licensee's license

Note: Convictions of driving while under the influence of drugs or alcohol are considered to be very serious by the Dental Board of California and a rigorous investigation will ensue to ensure the safety and welfare of their patients. Even allegations of DUI will warrant a substantial investigation by the Board.

Natural Disasters and Pandemic

No one ever expects that a hurricane will blow through your town, destroying everything in its wake. You have seen those images on the news of the devastation that has been left behind after a tornado had no mercy on anything in its path. The newscasters quickly tell you about the homes leveled and the families left homeless. But what you don't hear about are the countless number of businesses of all kinds that were also torn apart due to the unrelenting wind and water. They don't tell you about the building in which the dental office operates that will have to close down because all of the equipment was washed away by the storm. No. You don't hear about the number of business people who are left penniless when a natural disaster strikes.

As harrowing as this tale is and it may seem like an impossibility, nature has a mind of its own. You must be prepared. Throughout this book, the resounding theme has been preparation: reviewing contracts to be prepared; purchasing insurance to be prepared; envisioning your future – yes, to be prepared! Unfortunately, although you cannot physically prepare for a hurricane to destroy your x-ray equipment or for the government to shut down all businesses due to a global pandemic, you can be financially prepared to account for some of these worst-case scenarios that could occur.

For example, when on March 24th, the governor of Massachusetts where I practice dentistry mandated that all non-essential businesses were forced to be closed due to the COVID-19 health issue, many businesses immediately knew that this was the end for them. They did not have enough money in savings to cover their employees' salaries for an undetermined length of time, the government had not yet released Small Business Administration Pandemic Loans and any glimmer of reopening was possibly weeks if not months away. Ultimately, it has been months, still many patients are as skeptical about opening their mouths to a general dentist as dentists are about being exposed to the deadly virus.

For those who did not have a substantial amount of liquid capital, these are very trying times. As I talked about in Chapter 5, saving for retirement or the "end day" may be sooner for some than others. Depending upon their industry and age when the pandemic occurred, some business owners, not just dentists, had to make the difficult decision of closing up shop for good whether they were financially ready or not. Restaurants, small businesses, theater, the arts, entertainment, medical offices, and dental offices alike all are faced with the same situation which leaves them scratching their heads, asking the question, "why didn't I save more money or how can I salvage my business?" Not to minimize the financial impact that COVID-19 has had on the economy, but in reality, money is the least of our worries as many people struggle for their last breath and others grieve their loved ones.

Nevertheless, the current global situation has confirmed to me the necessity for continuing to learn, the need to develop a budget, a plan of action, and to value the life and career that I have. It has also reminded me that as bad as the financial situation may be, none of us are in this alone!

Epilogue

*Adding it all up;
The Dental dream and how you want to live*

"In five years, the Corleone family is going to be completely legitimate"
~ Al Pacino, The Godfather

"The woods are lovely, dark and deep,
But I have promises to keep,
And miles to go before I sleep,
And miles to go before I sleep"
~ Robert Frost - famous American poet

I hope you have found this guidebook helpful and a resource you will refer back to periodically. There is so much we as dental professionals are responsible for and so little we are prepared for when we start the journey. We seem to fit in a unique category of workers who must build their businesses without all the tools to do it. I sincerely hope this text has helped fill in some of the voids you have been searching for, and that you feel better prepared for tomorrow than you were yesterday.

In closing, I want to share a great piece of advice I read many years ago in Tim Ferris's book *The 4-Hour Workweek* that has helped shape my career and way of thinking. By no means am I saying you should follow it too nor that it's "right". But it is something worth digesting and perhaps considering applying to some aspect of your career or personal lives.

The concept is to plan your life in reverse: have an idea of what you want your future to be and start working towards that direction starting today rather than the other way around. Too often, we tend to allow our paths to be determined for us. Either from uncertainty, fear, or just laziness, it's easier to "go with the flow" and see what happens. But by always letting the river take you where it wants, you are at its mercy. Instead, map the route you want to take before going, and follow the paths of the river that work best for you.

What would be your ideal work schedule, salary, and lifestyle 5 years from now? What about 10 and 20? Do you want to travel the world often, or are you most content at home? Do you want to work 6 days a week or 4? Ask yourself questions and make a plan, no matter how outrageous some of your ideas may be. Then break each idea down into parts, calculate some relative costs, brainstorm how you could make the timing work, and see what is necessary to make it happen. The results may surprise you. Of course, this path can evolve and may likely alter some over time, but at least it will help provide some direction.

If your goal is to only work four days per week and travel constantly then buying a large practice with many chairs and at a massive debt to the bank makes that a difficult task. But having that same goal for ten to fifteen years from now might mean that option is the ideal way to go if you put in the hard work on the front end. It just depends on your individual plan and end game. The best part is that there are no wrong answers. Sounds obvious, but you would be surprised how many people lose track of the bigger picture.

Now I have had friends tell me that it's not realistic to plan this way if you already own a practice, or have kids, or are already in too much debt. But there are people with each, if not all of the situations combined, that still dictate their life and lifestyle on their terms. Some of it may be time management and skill, but in the end, it's a mentality that you control and you can decide how you want it to work in your favor.

Knowing when or if to purchase a practice is a big decision, and how you go about making that decision should continue to be based on a lot of due diligence and research. Remember that the banks ultimately care about your money, and not you. Also remember that banks base their decisions for everything you do in life based on the ***past***; past income, history, past credit, etc, but everything you are doing and preparing for is based for your ***future***. Thus, you need to look hard not only at the past but also at the present and your future. Ask yourself difficult questions and make honest calculations.

I am currently reading a great book by David Epstein called "Range- Why Generalists Triumph in a Specialized World". It demonstrates among other things how when we make calculations about ourselves or something we are directly familiar with, we tend to naturally increase the positive outcome;

when we believe in our specific cases, we will earn more money, do things quicker, better, and more efficiently than someone else in a similar situation. This is not because we are arrogant, but rather because we have familiarity with our own cases. Have a group of choices to choose from, and you will better rate the choice that you have familiarity with, even without knowing anything about the other options.

In this same context, the author shows with evidence that when planning for the outcome of a given project we are working on, we tend to give ourselves too much credit compared to others doing the same thing. You may know 5 other people trying to build an office from scratch, but in your estimation, your project will be done quicker, better and at a lower cost than the others because your knowledge of the specific details in your case make you believe your outcome will be better. I mention this simply to say that when planning for your future, and the potential purchase/acquisition of a practice, be realistic with yourself. Do not believe that your case is any more unique than what others in similar situations as you have had to deal with (in similar style cities, populations, etc).

Being overly optimistic may result in inaccurate calculations and inadvertently putting yourself in a precarious position. Look at both the best and the worst-case scenarios, run all the numbers, and see what they show. Will the worst-case scenario still cover your expenses and leave a little breathing room for emergency expenses and some pocket change for yourself? If so, great! If not, then it may be time to reconsider. This pandemic has been Exhibit A of the consequences.

It's also worth noting that with time, our priorities and opinions on things will also change. The author points out how long-term planning can actually *hinder* our overall final result and progress as it sets us on a linear and rigid path that we feel we can no longer stray away from. However, by being more flexible, and by often doing things through trial and error, over the short term, we can learn valuable lessons that help shape our direction and eventually influence our long-term outcome. Sometimes as dentists we fall into this trap as well, I know I have.

In other words, we are so goal-oriented and focused on a final product that we may miss a lot of great opportunities and experiences along the way by not keeping our eyes open to what's in our periphery as well. Food for thought.

Whatever you decide to do, remember to always ask yourself whether the decision you are contemplating will help get you closer to where you want to end up or pull you further away. Regardless of your journey, I wish you all the best of luck and great success in your dental adventures. And as my friend and dental colleague, Dr. Carmine Morreale always tells me, "Remember, you are not alone!"

APPENDIX

Dreamline

Tim Ferriss' *The 4-Hour Workweek*

Dreamline Worksheet

TIMOTHY FERRISS

The 4-Hour Workweek

DREAMLINE WORKSHEET

pg 1 of 2 »

In ___ months I **DREAM** of:

visit this blog post

HAVING

STAR?	DESCRIPTION	COST	COST TYPE
1			
2			
3			
4			
5			
	MONTHLY TOTAL	$0	

BEING

STAR?	DESCRIPTION	TO MAKE IT HAPPEN	COST	COST TYPE
1				
2				
3				
4				
5				
		MONTHLY TOTAL	$0	

DOING

STAR?	DESCRIPTION	COST	COST TYPE
1			
2			
3			
4			
5			
	MONTHLY TOTAL	$0	

Monthly Expenses (w/30% buffer): Go! $0

Target Monthly Income (TMI)	$0
Target Daily Income (TDI)	$0
TMI of Starred Items	$0
TDI of Starred Items	$0

Steps Now

1
2
3
4

Tomorrow

1
2
3
4

Day After

1
2
3
4

set consulting

TIMOTHY FERRISS

The 4-Hour Workweek

MONTHLY EXPENSE CALCULATOR

« pg 2 of 2

1. Where am I now? Input all of your current monthly expenses. If something doesn't fit in the below categories, add it into the "miscellaneous" total. This is a good snapshot of your outgoing cash-flow.

2. Where should I be? Subtract all non-essentials that are no longer used or used infrequently. Eliminate all things that consume income or attention without enriching your life (subscriptions to magazines you don't read, memberships to services you don't use, seldom-driven but often-serviced cars, etc.). This new end total, multiplied by 1.3 to provide a 30% buffer, is the clean slate that we take to the next step—adding in all the elements and luxuries that define your ideal lifestyle.

MONTHLY TOTALS	
Rent/Mortgage [1]	
Property Taxes	
Education/Tuition	
Credit Card Minimum Payments [2]	
Car Payments	
Other Loan Payments	
Car Insurance [1]	
Home Insurance	
Life Insurance	
Health/Dental Insurance	
Telephone	
Cable/TV	
Heating/Electricity	
Water	
Gasoline	
Public Transportation	
Groceries	
Eating Out	
Subscriptions (Online and Offline)	
Memberships	
Miscellaneous	
TOTAL SPENT FOR MONTH	$0.00
DREAMLINE BUFFER	$0.00

Fill out your Dreamline: 

[1] Once you begin taking mini-retirements, many of these expenses can be replaced by cheaper expenses overseas, whether for one month or 24 months. I [Tim Ferriss] saved more than $32,000 by traveling through 20 countries for 15 months as compared to just sitting at home in northern California. Extended travel or relocation to dream locations is actually a popular Lifestyle Design tactic for increasing savings.

[2] Whenever possible, look at credit card statements and put the expenses in other categories, as "credit cards" is too vague to be useful. This calculator should be used to determine exactly where you're spending income.

set consulting

Sample Dreamline

IN 6 MONTHS I DREAM OF:

	STEP 1: HAVING	STEP 5: COST
*	1. Aston Martin DB9	1. $2,003/month
	2. Go Board from 1800s	2.
*	3. Personal assistant	3. $5/hr. x 80 = $400
	4. Full Kendo armor	4.
	5.	5.
		A = $2,403

	STEP 2: BEING		STEP 4: DOING	STEP 5: COST
	1. flexible	→	1. full side splits	1.
*	2. best-selling author	→	2. sell 20,000 per week	2. $0 (3 free interns for media calls & own time)
	3. fluent in Greek	→	3. have 15-minute conversation w/native	3.
	4. excellent cook	→	4. make Thanksgiving dinner for six people	4.
	5.	→	5.	5.
				B = $0

	STEP 3: DOING	STEP 5: COST
	1. sell a TV show	1.
*	2. visit Croatian coast	2. $514 roundtrip airfare, $420 rent
	3. find smart & gorgeous girlfriend	3.
	4.	4.
	5.	5.
		C = $934

TARGET MONTHLY INCOME

A + B + C + (1.3 x monthly expenses)

=

TMI: $3,337 + ($2,600) = $5,937

÷ 30

=

TDI: $197.90

STEPS NOW

1. Find showroom, schedule test drive
2. Post bullet-point job description on 3 major sites
3. Send top 3 questions to five best-selling authors from 2–3 years ago
4. Visit Virtual Tourist and determine best season and to-do top 5

TOMORROW

1. Take test drive
2. Assign 1- to 2-hour task to top 3
3. Formulate plan around responses (marketing/PR)
4. Research tickets & housing for 3 weeks and invite friend to go

DAY AFTER

1. Decide on desired details & extras
2. Choose top 1 for 20 hrs. per week
3. Send intern recruitment e-mail to nearby college English departments
4. Reserve tickets (for yourself even if friend refuses)

Dreamline

(Go to www.fourhourworkweek.com for larger printable worksheets and online calculators.)

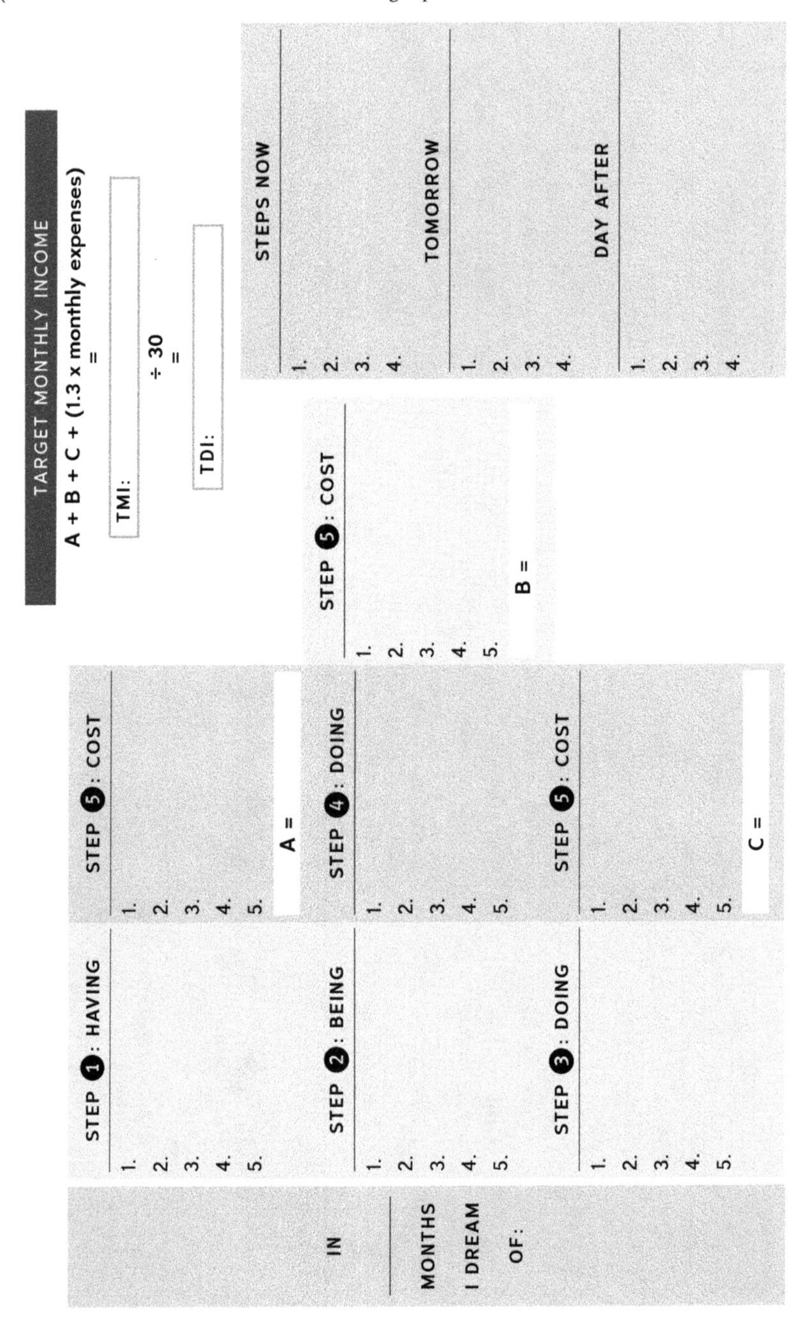

The Scary Reality

Having completed reading the book, let's take a look at a basic scenario using baseline estimated numbers to demonstrate the scary reality of life as an early career dentist. Again, the numbers are just approximate estimates, and of course, will vary in everyone's case, but it will show some of the costs and expenses to manage from day 1.

Yearly Gross Income - $200,000 (this puts you in the top 7% percentile of income in the US)

Net Income after taxes - $136,000 (Taxes in this bracket are 32%. You are therefore kissing away nearly $65k right off the bat)

Student Loan Debt - $400,000

Average per month costs:

- Student Loans - $4000 (this is the combined "suggested" payment amount found on your statements)
- Cost of Rent- $2000
- Utilities Cost- $350
- Auto Cost (Lease + gas + insurance) - $750
- Mobile Phone - $100
- Health Insurance - $250
- Disability Insurance - $100
- Malpractice Insurance - $85
- Professional Organizations (ADA, local dental society, etc) - $250

- Professional Assistance (CPA, Lawyers, Corporation Fees, etc) - $300
- Food and Drink - $750
- Miscellaneous expenses (shopping, pet fees, gym membership, Uber, etc) - $600
- Travel - $350

Savings Account/Retirement Contribution - ????

TOTALS:

PER MONTH EXPENSES: $9,885...let's say **$10,000** for easy math

PER YEAR EXPENSES: $120,000

OUR YEARLY NET *MINUS* OUR YEARLY EXPENSES - APPROX $16,000, OR $1,333.33/MONTH leftover profit

As you can see, despite earning an income which puts us in the top 7% of the country, with our baseline estimate of monthly expenses, we are left with about $16,000 "extra" at the end of the year.

Keep in mind, this does NOT include any money that we are planning to contribute to our retirement account (401k, IRA, SEP, etc) or that was already set aside each month by our employer. Include those numbers and you will realize that after a hard year's work as a dentist, you will look at your bank account and immediately ask yourself "where the hell is all my money?!"

It's a sobering feeling. Having seen this hypothetical example visually, I hope you can appreciate the need for good financial planning, and why leasing that BMW convertible and buying that new Rolex as a gift to yourself maybe is better left for a few years later when you are a bit more established.

Of course, depending on where you live, all the costs and income levels might vary quite a bit; a gallon of gas in California may cost double than most states. Regardless, sit down and make a similar list of your expenses and do *not* be conservative. Overestimate your expenses, including savings, and take into account your student loan situation and paying off that loan quicker. Maybe this example will help you realize you need to consider an income deferred program instead. Whatever your situation, don't be fooled about the economic realities and instead be prepared. However bleak it may appear, know that we all have had to go through it, and there is a light at the end of the tunnel, but proper planning is essential.

Join Our Community

Feel free to check us out on our website, www.fsg4dentists.com!

Find information about the book, sponsors, our new mentorship program, and become part of our community! Send us your feedback, apply to become a mentor, and let us know what additional content you would like us to provide. Together, we can help one another succeed!

Also, learn more about my revolutionary hearing protection product for dentists, EarAid!

EarAid

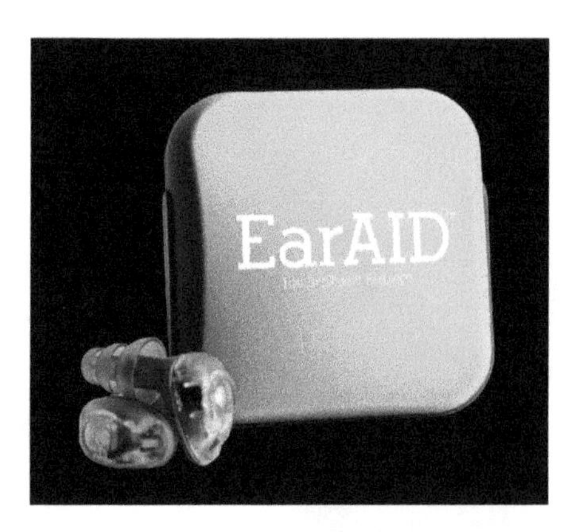

EarAid hearing protection product which if you haven't heard of before, you should seriously consider and look into on our website www.fsg4dentists.com

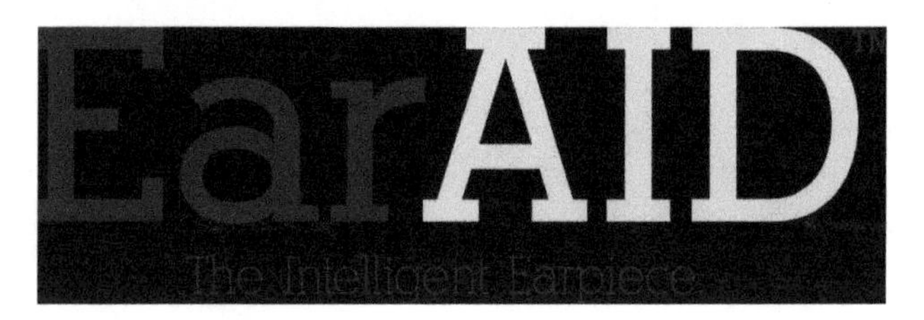

References

Student loan sample statement

https://www.nelnet.com/documents/marketing/pdf/Nelnet-Statement-Guide.pdf

Student loan options

https://www.salliemae.com/college-planning/student-loans-and-borrowing/compare-federal-vs-private-loans/

https://studentaid.gov/understand-aid/types/loans/plus/grad

Glossary terms

https://studentaid.gov/help-center/answers/topic/glossary/articles

Federal vs Private student loans

https://studentaid.gov/understand-aid/types/loans/federal-vs-private

Repayment options

https://studentaid.gov/understand-aid/types/loans/plus/grad#eligibility

https://studentaid.gov/manage-loans/repayment

https://www.finaid.org/loans/repayment.phtml

https://studentloanhero.com/featured/income-based-repayment-plan/

Prepayments

https://www.nerdwallet.com/article/loans/student-loans/pay-off-student-loans-fast

Refinancing/consolidation

https://studentloanhero.com/featured/repayment-student-loan-forgiveness-for-dentists-ultimate-guide/

https://www.nerdwallet.com/blog/loans/student-loans/student-loan-refinancing-faq/

https://www.sofi.com/learn/content/student-loan-refinance-denied/

Dental Employment Agreements: A Guide to Key Legal Provisions

https://ebusiness.ada.org/assets/docs/2502.pdf?orderid=400878

"A Dentist's Guide to Selecting a Lawyer"

https://ebusiness.ada.org/assets/docs/6850.PDF?OrderID=2104406

Small Business Tax Deductions

https://www.thebalancesmb.com/business-tax-deductions-from-a-to-z-397616

Taxation

https://www.bizfilings.com/toolkit/research-topics/managing-your-taxes/overview-of-tax-implications-of-llcs-and-corporations

Tax Cuts

https://www.whitecoatinvestor.com/pass-through-income-deduction/

Disability Insurance

www.policygenius.com Written by Collin Lalley

https://www.policygenius.com/disability-insurance/disability-insurance-definitions/

https://www.leveragerx.com/blog/occupation-classes-disability-insurance/

https://www.leveragerx.com/blog/level-vs-graded-disability-insurance-premiums/\

Retirement Planning

https://www.pbs.org/wgbh/frontline/film/retirement-gamble/

The 50/30/20 Rule - Elizabeth Warren and Amelia Warren Tyagi. "All Your Worth: The Ultimate Lifetime Money Plan." Simon & Schuster, 2005.

SEP IRA

https://www.investopedia.com/ask/answers/08/roth-traditional-sep.asp

Stock/bonds/mutual funds

https://www.thebalance.com/the-difference-between-stocks-and-bonds-417069

https://www.thebalance.com/should-you-invest-in-mutual-funds-or-stocks-3306145

Buying a dental practice

http://marketplace.ada.org/blog/the-real-cost-of-owning-a-dental-practice/

Letter of Intent

https://www.dentistryiq.com/practice-management/industry/article/16366617/the-first-step-toward-buying-a-practice-the-letter-of-intent

Steps to buying a practice

https://odgerslawgroup.com/buying-a-dental-practice-checklist/

Dental practice comparison figures

https://www.dentalclinicmanual.com/2-facilities/sec1-01.php

Staff's role in the sale of a business

https://www.dentistrytoday.com/hygiene/1183--sp-2051540979

Dental Demographics

https://dentagraphics.com/

Selecting a location

https://www.dentalstartupacademy.com/deciding-on-a-location-for-a-dental-office/

Overhead Budget

https://na.eventscloud.com/file_uploads/671823b21a962ff9d349ff281be06d5a_L106_Fettig-Benchmarks.pdf

https://www.dentistrytoday.com/news/todays-dental-news/item/2946-the-costs-of-starting-a-private-dental-practice

https://www.dentaleconomics.com/practice/overhead-and-profitability/article/16393116/you-choose-your-overhead

Owning property

https://www.dentaleconomics.com/practice/article/16386224/how-to-create-wealth-by-owning-your-office-location-and-other-real-estate

https://www.dentalcounsel.com/dentalandmedicalblog/in-a-dental-practice-owning-real-estate-has-advantages-over-leasing

Lawsuits

https://www.dentistrytoday.com/news/todays-dental-news/item/3737-how-lawsuits-can-damage-your-dental-practice

Bankruptcy

https://www.experian.com/blogs/ask-experian/credit-education/bankruptcy-how-it-works-types-and-consequences/

Criminal convictions

https://sethweinsteinlaw.com/dental-board-of-california-dental-license-discipline-for-dui/

Printed in the USA
CPSIA information can be obtained
at www.ICGtesting.com
LVHW021835191023
761417LV00044B/113/J